Finding God in the Midst of Life

Finding God in the Midst of Life

Old Stories for Contemporary Readers

Richard Bauckham and Trevor Hart

Paternoster:
thinking faith

LONDON ● ATLANTA ● HYDERABAD

12 11 10 09 08 07 06   7 6 5 4 3 2 1

First published 2006 by Paternoster
Paternoster is an imprint of Authentic Media
9 Holdom Avenue, Bletchley, Milton Keynes, Bucks,
MK1 1QR, UK
285 Lynnwood Avenue, Tyrone, GA 30290, USA
OM Authentic Media, Medchal Road, Jeedimetla Village,
Secunderabad 500 055, A.P., India
www.authenticmedia.co.uk
Authentic Media is a division of Send the Light Ltd., a company
limited by guarantee (registered charity no. 270162)

British Library Cataloguing in Publication Data

A catalogue record for this book is available from the
British Library

ISBN-13 978-1-84227-472-9
ISBN-10 1-84227-472-4

Design by James Kessell for Scratch the Sky Ltd
(www.scratchthesky.com)
Print Management by Adare Carwin
Printed and bound by J.H. Haynes & Co., Sparkford

Contents

Foreword

Stories have a special place in our lives. It has even been suggested that stories are what make us human, setting us apart from God's other sentient creatures. Perhaps this is stretching the point a little too far (lots of other things have a reasonable claim to be considered at that point); but it's surely fair to admit that stories are central to much of what matters to us humanly, to what makes our lives worth living. We instinctively tell stories, about ourselves and about others; and we love to hear stories told.

There's something about a good story (or any story for that matter) that sinks hooks easily, quickly and deep in our interest and reels us in. From Homer's *Iliad* to the latest plot of *Eastenders*, we find stories hard to resist, no matter how hard we may try. As accomplished communicators across the ages have all realized, no matter how profound or well-constructed an argument or exhortation may be, there's just no substitute for 'Once upon a time . . .' and its equivalents if you want to carry an audience with you and secure a sympathetic hearing.

No doubt there are lots of reasons for this. But one central reason has to do with the fact that stories are essential to the ways in which we make sense of our experience of life, our own lives as well as those of others. Stories, that is to say, are about finding and making meaning amidst the bits and pieces of our lives. A story, as we all know, has characters, and a beginning, middle and end. The matter is much more complicated than that, but that's enough already to indicate the way stories have to do with tracing connections between things – people, events, actions and outcomes. By telling stories, we link things together in patterns, suggesting that certain things belong naturally together, not just in the way that all the bits and pieces in a dustbin belong together (an accidental conglomeration of otherwise unrelated objects), but as part of a meaningful and orderly pattern. And by telling such stories about other people, of course, we get some sense of that unfolding story (as yet unfinished) that helps us make sense of our own life.

Stories, then, help us to locate ourselves within the complex web of the things that confront us as we live our lives. They help to situate us within what can otherwise be a bewildering interplay of like and unlike, familiar and unfamiliar, the reassuring and the threatening. Stories, in fact, are essential to our capacity to trace these differences and similarities, helping us to feel our way out imaginatively beyond the limits of our own particular place in the world and its history, while yet remaining earthed solidly within it. As C. S. Lewis puts it in his book *An Experiment in Criticism*, in reading a good story 'I become a thousand men and yet remain myself. . . . I transcend myself; and am never more myself than when I do.'[1] Stories, we might say, help us to grapple with the peculiar relationship between the particular and the shared in human experience: we only find stories interesting when they tell us things (about people, times, places, events) that we do not already know; yet we only find these things interesting and meaningful at all because we recognize them as human realities, things that might have been true of or experienced by us. We are drawn quickly into stories because, for all their possible strangeness, we can always find something of ourselves and our world in them.

The Bible is full of stories. Indeed, it is possible (and habitual) to view the collection of books that make up our Old and New Testaments as telling one big 'story'. The way in which the biblical books are organized within the Christian canon encourages us to approach it in this way, if not only in this way. And the first 'volume' or testament tells a particular part of that bigger story, narrating God's dealings with the people of Israel through Abraham, Jacob, Moses, Joseph, Samuel, David, and many, many others. Some of their stories are very familiar to us; others much less so. What all of them have in common, though, is that, in one way or another, God is a central player in the action which unfolds. Sometimes he is there openly and obviously. Sometimes his presence is more ironic, hidden and in need of interpretation (a sort of biblical 'Where's Waldo?'!). But, obvious or not, God is always there somewhere in the pattern of things; because the wider story which is being told is his story before it is Israel's story or ours. Indeed, given that these odd little stories themselves straddle many centuries and have their provenance in quite differing cultural and religious contexts, it is precisely the presence and the constancy of this one central divine 'character' that holds them all together, and makes them a proper part of the wider story of salvation.

Something similar is true of us and of our personal 'stories' of course. We discover that we, too, are characters in God's story, whether we like it or not; and God is thereby a character in ours. Again, this does not mean that God's presence or activity will always be as obvious as we might like. On other occasions, it may be far more apparent than we are comfortable with! Like the characters whose stories are included in this collection of meditations on Scripture, though, whether apparent or not, we are always called to look for and to find God in the midst of life's varying circumstances. Though the times and places of their encounters with this God were, in all manner of ways, very different to our own, there are things which straddle the differences. Time and time again the light of recognition dawns as our imagination is willingly taken captive, and we find ourselves translated across millennia and continents, face to face on the one hand with someone who bears an uncanny resemblance to us, and on the other with a God who, for all his elusiveness, is identifiably the same yesterday, today and forever.

Our thanks are due to those members of the congregation of St Andrew's Episcopal Church, St Andrews, who first heard the sermons on which these meditations are based. Thanks are due, too, to our good friend Micheal O'Siadhail for permission to cite his poem 'Twofold' from *Our Double Time* (Bloodaxe Books, 1998).

Richard Bauckham and Trevor Hart
Lent 2006

1

... in attempts to make God's promises manageable

(Genesis 16 and 21)

DIVORCED COUPLE FIGHT FOR FROZEN EMBRYOS . . .
(The Guardian, Saturday 6 November 1999)

The story which ran under this newspaper headline would, even a couple of decades ago, have stretched credulity to its limits and seemed better placed in science fiction than a reliable report of current affairs. Technological advance is too often presented as unalloyed progress whereas, as the newspaper story betrays, it frequently lifts the lid of a Pandora's Box, releasing ethical quandaries hitherto undreamed of even in our worst nightmares. The ancient story of Abraham, Sarah, Hagar and Ishmael, though, resonates eerily with the issues underlying this latter day dilemma. Of course there are patent differences between the situations the two stories describe, differences which warn us against reading ourselves and our way of seeing and doing things too quickly or easily into the biblical text. And yet, woven together with the differences, we may legitimately identify some deep flowing currents of shared humanity that straddle the millennia, and bring the ancient text to life for us as modern readers.

Both stories begin in the same place, a place that we will find in the geography of any human society we care to consider: there is a man and a woman who desire a child, but who, thus far, have been unable to have one, and for whom the sands of time seem to be running out. So they devise a strategy for resolving the problem. Of course, frozen embryos are entirely foreign to the Bible's world, and the complex moral dilemmas associated with modern infertility treatments are not readily transposed across the centuries. But Abram and Sarai have their own – crude but in biological terms equally efficient – 'technology' to hand in the form of Hagar the slave girl, whose fertility is apparently not in dispute. Surrogacy does not wait for the invention of the test tube. The ancients had their own way of doing it. It may seem to us to be an unsatisfactory state of affairs in moral terms; but morality in this whole area is a fragile thing, and those who live in glasshouses ought not to throw stones too quickly. In any case, that's not where either of the stories concentrates our attention as readers. Neither of them has any direct interest in the *moral* rights and wrongs of the technology: they are concerned rather with the complications that arise in human relationships as a result of its deployment. This, it seems, is another feature of human life ancient and modern alike: the attempt to 'play God' where the conception of new life is concerned, whatever its rights and wrongs, has some unlooked for and unwelcome fallout. It seems that the process inevitably ends up generating some human surplus; in relationships, in expectations and in actual flesh and blood. And it's not easy to know what to do with this surplus once the process has generated its initially desired result.

If we turn to the biblical story as we pick it up initially in Genesis 15, we may notice first the immediate context for it. Abram has been beseeching God for an heir, worried that his family heritage will otherwise be passed on to a slave in his household, Eliezer of Damascus. So God makes a promise to Abram: '"This man shall not be your heir, your own son shall be your heir." And he brought him outside and said, "Look toward heaven, and number the stars, if you are able to number them." Then he said to him, "So shall your descendants be."' (15:4-6) When Abram comes home, excitedly, and tells Sarai about this, it's not likely that she shares his enthusiasm. More likely, the whole idea serves to dump an enormous load of pressure and guilt on her. She is old, and thus far infertile. The opening verse of our passage casts her pretty much in this mould, as a worthy but biologically unfruitful wife: 'Now Sarai, Abram's wife, bore him no children' (16:1). So what, then, is to be done? Abram wants children. That's natural enough, not least in a society whose economic fabric and welfare mechanisms are more closely tied to biological relationships than in our own. We aren't told, but may suppose that Sarai too would rather like to have had a family. But that abiding pressure, which has built up over so many years of hopeful waiting and watching as the biological clock ticked its way toward and then past the menopause, is now increased to the 'nth' degree by the heavy theological spin put on matters by Abram. 'Oh by the way Sarai, God told me today that he will provide us with a son; a whole constellation of them in fact.' It's Abram's (and God's) bright idea, but the way Sarai sees it, it places *her* in a position of some responsibility for coming up with the goods! And while Abram seems able contentedly to trust God, Sarai isn't so sure. She really can't believe that the plan can involve her in conceiving and bearing a child at her age. That's too much even to imagine. Maybe it's something she doesn't actually *want* to imagine! So, she comes up with what must seem to her a workable route to achieving the goal, but without demanding anything quite so miraculous. She engages in a significant downsizing of imagination. She is old, and it 'has ceased to be with her after the manner of women'. But she has a young Egyptian slave girl who does just about everything else for her around the house, so why not this? All it needs is for Abram to sleep with the girl until she becomes pregnant (a scheme with which Abram, for all his willingness to trust God, nonetheless seems happy to go along . . .), and the child can be raised in the household as his heir. All the pressure will be taken off Sarai herself, and the focus upon her own inadequacy finally shifted.

So Sarai takes responsibility for getting Abram the son he so desires, and the host of descendants God has promised him. It's a cunning plan. But it's a plan with a serious flaw. You see, even though Sarai is seeking to secure what God has said will happen, her energies are invested in getting things done in *her* way, securing herself from what she fears might otherwise come about: either failure, disappointment and shame, or else pregnancy with its attendant risks and worries at her stage in life. For Sarai, God's promise is not sufficient. She cannot sit around waiting to see how and when God might begin acting on that promise. She wants the security of *knowing* how and when, indeed of *controlling* how and when, it will all happen. She's not yet ready to deal with God on his terms, but wants to have a hand in some sort of negotiation with him. 'Okay God, you want to achieve X, but frankly it's as clear as houses that factor Y is missing from the equation here, so I think we should go down route Z, and then we'll have a reasonable chance of success between the two of us.' Here, if ever, we can properly say that a bid to heal the pain of infertility amounts to 'playing God'. But Sarai, the one who laughs at God's outrageous promise, still has to learn that *nothing* is too wonderful for the LORD. Her action is in fact a form of faithlessness, immersing herself in activity allegedly for God and his purposes, but in reality refusing to face the implications of who God really is in her own life at this point. It's a faithlessness of which Sarai is cured later in her story; but for now God lets her get on with it, and learn the hard way; because it is this same 'reasonable' and manageable strategy that causes her and others so much heartache and bitterness in what follows.

There's no suggestion in the story that there is anything exceptional about the surrogacy arrangement as such, although from a slave girl's perspective it is always likely to feel like going beyond the call of duty! But in the story Hagar's feelings about the matter are left unreported, until the point where she discovers that she is indeed pregnant with Abram's child. And then, we read, 'she looked with contempt on her mistress'. It's a highly charged phrase that conveys a lot in very few words. Hagar cannot quite cope with the social dislocation that puts her, a slave girl, in her master's bed; not furtively, as one used for fun and then cast aside, but openly, under her mistress's instruction, and because she has something to offer Abram that Sarai herself, for all her wealth and social graces, cannot supply. No wonder, then, that when her body comes up with the goods, and her pregnancy is announced, Hagar feels a certain sense of triumph. It's not every day that the tables are turned so blatantly between slave and owner; and even though this whole thing was Sarai's own idea, its success carries an ironic sting in its tail for her. Putting another woman into her husband's bed, and then seeing the ease with which she tumbles into pregnancy when she, Sarai, has waited so many long years, month after aching month to no avail, all of this has more than merely physical and biological dimensions. And, far from relieving her of a sense of inadequacy, it serves only to reinforce that sense. That the problem was hers all along is now clear for all to see. And the contemptuous gaze of her own slave girl, following her around the room, no doubt simply rubs salt deep into the open wound in Sarai's soul, until she cannot bear it. This, then, is where things begin to turn sour in the story. Sarai, doing what she believed to be best for her husband and her marriage, now feels effectively displaced as a wife, a judgement that Hagar's gradually swelling belly throws back in her face tenfold and for all to see.

When Sarai confronts Abram with all this he is at least able to reassure her that he has come through the surrogacy thing emotionally unscathed. He has formed no romantic attachment or inclinations with respect to Hagar whatsoever. 'She is your slave girl. Do with her as you like.' It's not one of the more touching moments in the story! But Sarai takes him at his word, and immediately sets about putting Hagar back in her place, making it unequivocally clear that her role as human test tube changes absolutely nothing so far as power relationships within the household are concerned. And, we read, 'she treated her harshly' (16:6).

The text passes quickly over what we may surmise must be a brutal and cruel episode, for it is sufficient to drive Hagar, pregnant and with no alternative means of support or survival, not only out of Abram's bed, but out of his household and into the desert with all its perils. Where did she think she was going, out here in the middle of nowhere? She probably didn't have a clue, hadn't even thought about it. As so often when pain and hurt of one sort or another become unbearable, we run simply to get away from the cause, and don't stop to think about the direction in which we are heading. And it's here, we are told, that 'the angel of the LORD found her' (16:7), resting beside a spring of water. Notice how the angel's words force her to reckon with the question of her own proper place in Abram's household, and to face what has happened to her: 'Hagar, slave-girl of Sarai, where have you come from and where are you going?' (16:8) Hagar must have begun to feel a bit unsure about that in recent days. From slave girl to bedmate to the expectant mother of her mistress's husband, all within so short a space of time. But then, just as suddenly,

dumped back into the stark reality of all that slavery really means
in its worst moments – treated to a verbal (and perhaps even a
physical) barrage of demeaning proportions until she could stand
it no longer. We may wonder, amidst that torrent, just how many
times the words 'who do you think you are?!!' were screamed at
her by Sarai? Could Hagar have answered them? After all, who
was she now? Slave? Mistress? Rape victim? Wife? Scheming trol-
lop? Mother? Rival for Abram's love? Rival for his inheritance?
She hadn't asked for any of this. She hadn't craved it or sought it.
It had been thrust upon her whether she liked it or not. Whoever
she had once been, a lot had happened to change things, and now
she needed some clear reaffirmation of who she was, who she
could feel free to *be* without feeling guilty. So the angel's words are
highly charged: 'Hagar, slave girl of Sarai, where have you come
from? And where are you going?' They are words that confirm
and challenge, establish and interrogate, all in the same breath.
And they are words designed to begin to restore the broken order
of things resulting from Sarai's attempt to play God. Hagar *is*
Sarai's slave: not her rival; nor her equal; nor a substitute for her.
And it is fitting for her to return now and submit to Sarai, to take
up again her proper place in Abram's household.

But, of course, things can never be quite the same again. They
are all going to have to live with one very apparent consequence
of the ill-judged *ménàge à trois*. The child quietly growing in
Hagar's womb is not going to go away: and it has Abram's DNA
in its make-up, may well turn out to have his eyes, his laugh, his
cough, or his weakness for klezmer tunes. The child, in short, will
be identifiably *his* son, a part of him. Nothing can change that.
And that's not going to be easy to cope with; because the child
will *never* be Sarai's son, never *their* son. On the contrary, he will
be a piece of living shrapnel in the scar tissue of their relationship, disfiguring their shared remembering of this painful past,
and no doubt keeping Sarai's resentment against Hagar from
growing cold for many years to come. It's a tangled and even a
frightening prospect from Hagar's point of view. Surely, the best
thing would be either for her to keep running now and avoid the
whole protracted mess, or else for the pregnancy to come to some
convenient end. In her despair, perhaps Hagar even prays for a
miscarriage to remove the unsought and unwanted cause of all

her trouble. In our day, no doubt, she would be urged to think long and hard about the benefits of the 'morning after' pill, or how to scrape together enough cash to pay for a visit to a discreet private clinic in order to deal with the situation.

But there's been enough playing God already in this story, and the angel's words make it plain that even this flesh-and-blood reminder of a disruption in the proper order of things can be redeemed. God can bring blessing even out of our stupidest ideas and their consequences. So, in the midst of her loneliness, confusion and rejection, Hagar receives God's promise; a promise which sounds very much like that given to Abram, but which, as we discover only later in the story, is *not* the same promise at all, but one made to Hagar herself in her own right. This blessing is, as it were, sheer grace rather than utility. Sarai and Abram have tried to use Hagar in order to secure God's promised blessing. God will still grant the blessing, in his time, and in his surprising way. But *he* does not plan to use Hagar to do so. She, and this whole messy situation, are in one sense surplus to God's requirements, a complication not of his making, a gratuitous by-product of Sarai's lack of faith in God; but one that God is nonetheless able and willing to redeem and to bless. Ishmael will be the father of a multitude so great as to be incapable of being counted. There's a marvellous irony in this. God, as it were, both does and does not play into the hands of Sarai's carefully devised scheme. Hagar gets pregnant, as planned. She produces a son and heir for Abram, as planned. This son, it seems, will indeed be the father of multitudes in accordance with God's promise to Abram. God, as Ishmael's name proclaims, has indeed heard all that has been going on, and has responded. So, to all appearances, Sarai's scheme has worked.

Ishmael is duly born into Abram's household, and lives as Abram's son and heir for a full 13 years. And, although there are no doubt extra tensions, strains and stresses around the house as Ishmael grows from infancy to adolescence under Sarai's jealous gaze, all is nonetheless going fairly smoothly until, in Abram's ninety-ninth year, something quite unexpected and almost unthinkable happens. Sarai (who by now has become Sarah, and who has also, of course, grown older rather than younger in the intervening few verses) discovers that she is pregnant!! This is the divine spanner thrown into the carefully oiled works, God's grace interrupting our godless schemes in the most awkward and uncomfortable way, and reminding us of the cost of every self-reliant attempt to displace him from the centre of things. Despite God's accommodation of Ishmael, Isaac, the true heir, the fulfilment of the promise to Abram, is finally about to make an appearance in chapter 21, on God's terms, and in God's time and God's way.

Despite what they decided to call the baby, we may well doubt whether Hagar laughed much when she heard of Sarah's pregnancy, or at Isaac's birth. While everyone else at the party to mark the child being weaned was celebrating, Hagar was almost certainly finding it hard to enter fully into the spirit of things. This was anything but a good day so far as she was concerned. After all, the only thing granting her any distinction in Abraham's eyes or his household – the fact that she was the mother to his sole son and heir – had been rudely taken from her by circumstance. She could easily, and no doubt already feared that she might, in one way or another now be pushed aside together with her son as an unfortunate, inconvenient, perhaps even a threatening intrusion into the life of the newly reconfigured happy family.

Ishmael himself, though, seems unaware of any such scenario, and, thrilled with the novelty of Isaac, sets adolescent concerns about what is 'cool' temporarily aside to dandle the baby on his knee, gurgling and cooing without inhibition. And it's this sight, of Ishmael's natural and unselfconscious love for and enjoyment of her infant son, that lights a fire under Sarah's 13-year-old sense of rivalry and resentment, and brings it to the boil. The text unashamedly reflects her jaundiced perspective when it refers to Ishmael as 'the son of Hagar the Egyptian', conveniently forgetting for the moment that he is also Isaac's big brother. Whether Sarah's next action is sheer reflex (provoked by emotions long harboured in her soul, and now more than she can reasonably deal with any longer) or an opportunistic grasping of the excuse she has been waiting for, it is difficult to say. Is it just mercenary calculation that causes her to act, ensuring the whole inheritance will go to Isaac rather than being shared with his (already adolescent and rapidly approaching the age of inheritance) elder half-brother, or is there also jealousy and spite, perhaps even fear that even yet the Egyptian woman and her son may succeed in replacing her in Abraham's affections? We aren't told, and from Hagar's perspective it hardly matters. The practical result is the same either way. 'Cast out this slave woman with her son' (21:10), Sarah tells Abraham. And, although it hurts him to have to do so (Ishmael is, after all, *his* son too, and his firstborn), Abraham sees that this is probably the shrewdest course of action. His distress at the loss of his child, and his fear for the well-being of both the boy and his mother, is assuaged by God's promise: 'Don't be distressed: let them go. It is through Isaac that the promise will be fulfilled' (21:12), 'And I will look after Ishmael'. And, as he has in the past, despite the apparent consequences of doing so, and the way it is bound to appear to others, Abraham trusts God, packs up what few provisions the two can carry between them, and sends them out, bearing the unbearable consequences of Sarah's past with them into the wilderness.

They wander around, having nowhere and no-one to go to until, before long, their supply of water runs out. And then, as they gradually grow weaker and weaker – in a scene which we can easily imagine because it is so depressingly familiar from our TV screens – the broken-hearted mother sets her dehydrated son under what little shade from the sun she can find and waits for death to take him. And it's now, in the very depths of her rejection and loss, as she is forced to listen to the frightened cries of her dying child, that Hagar rediscovers the promise God had made to her during her earlier brush with the wilderness; a promise that breathes life into a situation otherwise laden with death and hopelessness; a promise she has all but forgotten and has to be reminded of. '"Come, lift up the boy and hold him fast with your hand, for I *will* make a great nation of him." Then God opened her eyes and she saw a well of water. She went, and filled the skin with water, and gave the boy a drink' (21:18). And so Hagar's story turns out to have a happy ending after all, even if the hurts and injustices of her experience in Abraham's household remain largely unresolved. And, ironically, despite his experience there Ishmael grew up to like the wilderness, and remained there for the rest of his life, all 137 years of it. In due course his mother made sure he married a nice girl from 'home', and – so chapter 25 tells us – he duly became the patriarch of 12 tribes who dwelt from Havilah to Shur. But the most important thing by far is already told us in Genesis 21:20. God was with him. Interestingly, it seems that the bitterness and rivalries were not passed on from mother to son. And when Abraham died, we read 'Isaac *and* Ishmael buried him together, in the cave of Machpelah . . . with his wife Sarah' (25:9). Even the most deep-seated and bitter of family feuds are not destined inevitably to incubate and fester across the generations, but can be redeemed when the living God is allowed into the midst of them.

This story reminds us that we should be wary of acting as though we can supply better strategies for achieving God's purposes for us than God himself can. That's something we are very prone to do, though often we won't be aware of doing or having done it. When the promise or command of God comes to us, we hear it clearly enough, but we don't pause to ask how we should proceed in pursuing it. Instead, we hurry straight out to pursue what seems to us to be the most obvious route. Or perhaps, like Sarai, our imagination is stretched to breaking point by what we hear, and we find it difficult to believe that God will actually do for and with us what at first blush he seems to be promising; so we scale things down to a more manageable size, fitting our expectations within the limits of credulity and human capacity. And again, having done so we rush ahead in pursuit of our more manageable schemes and less ambitious goals, drawing on our own resources and tacitly assuming the role of site manager in the construction of our own lives. The cautionary note in this story is that God may well let us do precisely this; but we may then have to live a long time (perhaps for the rest of our lives) with the consequences. God can redeem any mess we care to make in our lives, but it might be more prudent to stop at the outset and take stock of the situation. We need to trust God enough not only to receive the promises he makes, but to allow him to work in and through us at every juncture towards their realization, and in his way rather than ours, even (no, *especially*) when the promises seem to reach so far beyond the bounds of probability or reasonable expectation as to be laughable.

Lord of life,
who called the world into existence out of nothing,
who blessed Sarah's womb in her old age,
who filled Mary's womb though she knew not yet a man,
who broke open the tomb and raised your crucified Son to life on
    the third day,
who has promised to make all things new,
when your promises stretch our imaginations to the limit
grant us the faith to receive them and to trust you for their
    fulfilment.
    Amen.

. . . in the loneliness of life's journey

(Genesis 28:10-22)

Jacob is one of those Old Testament people who, even though he played a key role in God's purposes for the whole world, was also remarkably like ourselves, not living in a spiritual stratosphere where we could never imagine ourselves, but living through the ordinary experiences of life. Like us, Jacob sometimes makes a go of things and sometimes makes a mess of things. What is so encouraging for us is that Jacob finds in the course of his life that, unworthy of God though he is, God is in all these varied experiences with him, making in the end a decisive difference.

Our story in Genesis 28 tells how Jacob first found God as his own God. This was not the first that Jacob knew about God. He had grown up in a family where God was central to life, but up to this point he had known God precisely as the family's God – his father Isaac's God, his grandfather Abraham's God. This is why, when God speaks to Jacob in his dream, God introduces himself as 'the God of Abraham your father and the God of Isaac,' but does so in order to tell Jacob that now he is also to be Jacob's God. It is not coincidental that this happens at this precise point in Jacob's life. At the beginning of our story Jacob has for the first time in his life left the family home. In fact, he is fleeing for his life because his brother Esau is so angry with him Jacob is afraid Esau might kill him. His mother, who helped to get Jacob into this predicament, has packed him off, for his own safety, on a very long journey to the home of her relatives 500 miles away as the crow flies – a daunting journey into a quite unknown future. For the first time in his life Jacob is really on his own. So his relationship to God has to change if it is to be real for him now. Jacob, if he is to find himself apart from his family, if he is to find who he can now be in this newly uncertain world in which he is now alone, must also find God as his own God, God with him in this new independence in which he must learn to be himself afresh.

Not that Jacob thinks of this for himself. It is not Jacob who turns to God, but God who turns to Jacob. It happens in a dream. This is something you may or may not be able to relate to. Most of us most of the time take no notice of our dreams. We rarely even remember them, and unless we are into some kind of psycho-analysis we usually do not even try to remember them. But just now and then a dream has such an effect on us it stays with us. We might have just two or three strangely significant dreams in our life, dreams that seem to speak directly and intensely movingly to where we are at that point in my life, and so stay with us until we actually find, only from the way our life later develops, the significance of those dreams come to fruition. That is the kind of dream Jacob had, only more so. It was a dream that filled his mind when he awoke, gave him a new vision of his life, and stayed with him for the rest of his life. It was a dream in which God spoke to him. Whatever the function of most of our dreams, the unremembered ones, might be – the experts are still not really sure about that – we can see why God might, on occasion, speak to someone in a dream. A dream has that strange potential for making us feel, consciously, some of those deepest feelings we might not let ourselves feel in waking consciousness. Sometimes, even if unusually, a dream can tell us something about where we are at a critical moment in our lives. Perhaps God spoke to Jacob in a dream because it was the way God could address what Jacob was as yet barely conscious of: his new-found aloneness and uncertainty, the newly open future he had never had to face before. God not only spoke in the dream, but also gave Jacob a dream image – a picture with the kind of quality most of us experience only in dreams. It was an image that could stay with Jacob and shape his imagination, an image of what God was now to be for Jacob in the rest of his life.

We should probably not ponder our dreams every morning to see if we can find this kind of meaning in them. It is doubtful whether most dreams mean anything worth attending to. The significant ones are surely the ones we do not even have to try to remember. The rare dream in which God may speak to us will be unmistakable when it happens, just as it was for Jacob. But we need not count on having such a dream, for God speaks to us in many different ways. God gives us life-shaping images in many different ways. We need not expect a dream from God, though we might get one. We should expect to find God in the midst of our lives in whatever way God chooses to encounter us.

The image Jacob sees in his dream is probably not, as most of the translations have it, a ladder, but a staircase. We do not have to picture the angels on a ladder, pushing past each other rather dangerously as some climb up and others down. The Hebrew word can just as well mean a stairway. Most likely Jacob saw a broad stone staircase running up the stepped side of one of the artificial mountains – called ziggurats – that the ancient people of Mesopotamia used to build. The gods were thought to live at the top of the cosmic mountain that touches heaven. So, in order to worship them in a temple, the people of Mesopotamia would build a great mound and place the temple of the gods on the top of it, so that the gods could dwell there too, and the people could worship the gods by ascending the steps up the mound to its summit. If Jacob recognized this image, as well he might since his grandfather came from Mesopotamia, he would naturally look for God at the top of the stairway. But the remarkable thing about Jacob's dream is that God is not at the top of the stairway but at the bottom. God is standing beside him. Jacob does not have to make the arduous ascent up the stairway to God. Nor does he need to rely on the angels to put him in communication with God, acting as messengers. No, God himself has come down the staircase and stands looking down at Jacob sleeping beside him.

So when God speaks to Jacob what are really the key words in what he has to say to Jacob – 'I am with you' – he means it. God is not remote in heaven but down on earth with Jacob. And when Jacob wakes in wonder, the dream still filling his consciousness, and says, 'This is none other than the house of God,' he means: God's house, where God is to be found, is not only up in heaven, but here on this very spot where I have been sleeping. So he sets up his stone pillow as a pillar to mark the location of God's house, and calls it Bethel, which means 'God's house'. But even this does not reach the deepest meaning of the dream. Only symbolically does the place remain a reminder of God's presence there. Really God's presence is not localized in one place. The point of the dream is not so much that God is in that particular place, but that God is where Jacob is. God is with Jacob, and will be with him wherever he goes: 'Know that I am with you and will keep you wherever you go' (28:15). God's message to Jacob is not for a man who is going to settle down at Bethel with a temple close at hand in which to worship God. God's message is for a man on a journey. From now on every place where Jacob sleeps will be a Bethel. The leitmotif of Jacob's life from now on will be that God is with him. God is now his God.

Jacob finds that God is with him. It is probably the most important thing anyone can discover. It will make all the difference to Jacob's life.

It will be worth reflecting a little more on two aspects of the way Jacob finds God – or God finds Jacob – at this juncture of his life. The first is the fact that it happens when Jacob is near the beginning of a long, hazardous journey, whose outcome he cannot be sure of. Like all travellers in those days, Jacob has no map. He knows where he is going but probably has only a vague idea of how to get there. He has to keep asking the way at every stage of his journey. Even more important, he does not know what will happen to him when and if he reaches his cousins several hundred miles away. A journey in space is always also, of course, a journey in time. What is now so uncertain for Jacob is the future. Facing this open and rather frightening future is a new situation for him. He has always thought he can manage the future, be a success, making sure, by swindling his brother, that he can ensure the future will be just what he wants it to be. Now he faces a future he cannot control.

The fact that journeys in space are always also journeys in time is the reason why people have often thought of life as a journey. Life is a journey for which we do not have a map – an unsettling situation to contemplate. We may find it exciting or paralysing. One way of reacting is to think of the future as the wide open sphere in which we can make of ourselves and our lives whatever we choose. We can plan the future and achieve it. This is the ideology of modernity, with its tremendous faith in our ability to achieve and to control. It has an important element of truth, but it refuses to recognize the way our future is made at least as much by what happens to us, beyond our control, as by what we do ourselves. In fact, much of the joy of life comes, not from what we achieve, but from what we are given, what comes to us with the unexpectedness and the undeserved delight of sheer gift.

Another way we can react to being on a journey without a map is to give up the whole idea of travelling anywhere. The ideology of post-modernity denies that our lives can make sense as a story that moves from beginning to end. Life is just a series of fragments, a series of presents in which and with which we can play without thinking of the future. Life is transience but not journey. Nothing lasts and we are going nowhere.

Jacob, finding God with him, finds that although the future is unknown – since he has no map for the journey – two things are certain. One is that wherever he goes God will be with him. The second is that God will fulfil his promises to him. His future is not in his own hands but in those of the living and loving God who has now become Jacob's God.

So Jacob's story invites us to see our own lives as a journey with God. But there is also a second aspect of Jacob's experience that we need to consider. Jacob, sleeping on his stone pillow, is alone. In one sense being alone was not unusual for Jacob. He was a shepherd; he must have spent a lot of time out in the fields with only his flock for company. But at Bethel Jacob is alone in a much stronger sense, suddenly bereft of all the relationships that had made up his life until now. Losing the security of the loving family environment he had known all his life, Jacob has now no one to turn to. Does there have to be this aloneness – which is not necessarily loneliness – for there to be a Bethel experience of God?

The story points us to a very important aspect of discovering that God is with us. There is a kind of fundamental aloneness that each of us has and that is part of what it means to be human. It is something always true of us. You do not have to be alone in the ordinary sense to be alone in this fundamental sense, though you may have to be alone as Jacob was in order to realize this fundamental truth of the human condition. The point is that in even the most intimate of human relationships, when people enter very deeply into each other's lives, still there is a degree to which who I am is inaccessible to you and who you are is inaccessible to me. That is the fundamental human aloneness which even when we come closest to each other we do not lose and cannot lose. Some people spoil their deepest relationships by trying to dissolve this fundamental aloneness. It cannot be done. Some people find this fundamental aloneness terrifying and spend their lives trying not to be aware of it. But that only produces a shell of a life with a hidden emptiness at its core.

However, this solitary core of our human being, though inaccessible to other human beings, is not inaccessible to God. It is part of what it is for God to be God that he can be present in the innermost reality of each of his creatures, where they cannot be present to each other. It is there, in his inescapable aloneness, that God promises to be with Jacob. For many people, it is in an experience of aloneness like Jacob's that they find themselves in the presence of God. The experience is one in which one cannot evade but has to face up to that fundamental aloneness that is actually a basic truth about being human. We may not be physically alone like Jacob, but something happens to expose that solitary core of our being, the aloneness that no human relationship can abolish. We realize, as someone put it, 'that there is no one who is always going to be there for me.' Even in the best of families, the best of marriages, the best of friendships, in the end we must still recognize that 'there is no one who is always going to be there for me.' In the transient relationships our contemporary society fosters, in the culture of not wanting to be committed, not wanting to be tied down, wanting always to be free to be on the move again, many people glimpse the fundamental aloneness of the human condition and take refuge from it in transience, living on the convivial surface of life. But if that aloneness becomes the Bethel where we find God with us, then the God we may have known only as Abraham's God, Isaac's God, becomes Jacob's God, my God, your God, the God who is with us as no one else can be.

This may sound very individualistic. It is and it isn't. No one else's head can lie on Jacob's stone pillar while he dreams the dream we are trying to share. But the God each of us must come to know as our own God, not just the God of other people, is then also the

God we share with other people. The God we find in our fundamental aloneness is also the God we then find in every experience,
in every relationship, in all of the world God has created and fills.
Jacob was to find that too, later. When we find God as Jacob did at
Bethel, we can stop trying to fill our inner emptiness with people
and things instead of God. We can start really loving people.

Bethel was just the beginning of Jacob's journey with God. So
far as we can tell, nothing has changed in Jacob's character. He is
still the schemer who tricked his brother out of his birthright and
blessing. He has still got to face up to the mess he has made of his
family life. Later (in the story Genesis tells) he will. But he could
never have done so had he not first found God's sheer grace in
promising to be with him. God does not say to him at Bethel: If
you reform, I will be with you. Or, I will be with you so long as
you behave better than you have been behaving. God says simply: 'I *am* with you and I *will* keep you wherever you go.' Jacob
has a long way to go, but from this Bethel onwards God is in it
with him and that will make all the difference.

Jesus promised his disciples a Bethel experience. He said, 'You
will see the heavens opened and the angels of God ascending and
descending upon the Son of man' (John 1:51). In other words,
Jesus himself will be for his disciples the staircase linking heaven
and earth. Not just the staircase on which they can ascend to
heaven, but the staircase on which God has come down among
us. Jesus is the incarnation of God with us, and to find Jesus is to
find God with us in the midst of our lives.

Francis Thomson's poem, *In No Strange Land*, expounds the
theme that our Bethel may be wherever we are:

> O world invisible, we view thee,
> O world intangible, we touch thee,
> O world unknowable, we know thee,
> Inapprehensible, we clutch thee!
>
> Does the fish soar to find the ocean,
> The eagle plunge to find the air –
> That we ask of the stars in motion
> If they have rumour of thee there?
> Not where the wheeling systems darken,

And our benumbed conceiving soars! –
The drift of pinions, would we hearken,
Beats at our own clay-shuttered doors.

The angels keep their ancient places; –
Turn but a stone, and start a wing!
'Tis ye, 'tis your estrangd faces,
That miss the many-splendoured thing.

But (when so sad thou canst not sadder)
Cry; – and upon thy so sore loss
Shall shine the traffic of Jacob's ladder
Pitched betwixt Heaven and Charing Cross.

Yea, in the night, my Soul, my daughter,
Cry, – clinging Heaven by the hems;
and lo, Christ walking on the water
Not of Genesareth, but Thames!¹

. . . in doing what we can

(1 Samuel 17)

At chapter 17 we are about halfway through the book we call 1 Samuel, and at the point where the major theme of 1 Samuel is coming into clear view after the background and preliminaries to it. This theme is David's rise to power in Israel. While 2 Samuel is the story of David's rule as king of Israel, 1 Samuel is the story of how he got to be king. From the perspective of 1 Samuel the story is more precisely of the way God brought to power over his people the man God had chosen to rule his people, the 'man after [God's] own heart' as Samuel calls David at one point (1 Sam. 13:14), the man who could, as it were, exercise God's own rule over his people on God's behalf. The account of David's fight with Goliath in chapter 17 is doubtless the best-known episode in this story of David's rise to power, but to read it in context we need to understand how 1 Samuel presents God's purpose in giving David rule over his people. It does this initially, near the beginning of the book, in the song of Hannah (2:1-10), which, as well as belonging to the story of Hannah herself and her son Samuel, forms a kind of theological preface to the rest of the story the book will recount.

The song describes who the God is who is going to be active in the story of David, what kinds of things this God does, what sort of purposes this God has in view:

> There is no Holy One like the LORD,
>> no one besides you;
>> there is no Rock like our God.

Talk no more so very proudly,
let not arrogance come from your mouth;
for the LORD is a God of knowledge,
and by him actions are weighed.
The bows of the mighty are broken,
but the feeble gird on strength.
Those who were full have hired themselves out for bread,
but those who were hungry are fat with spoil.
The barren has borne seven,
but she who has many children is forlorn.
The Lord kills and brings to life;
he brings down to Sheol and raises up.
The LORD makes poor and makes rich;
he brings low, he also exalts.
He raises up the poor from the dust;
he lifts the needy from the ash heap,
to make them sit with princes
and inherit a seat of honor (1 Sam. 2:2-8a).

This God is the incomparable one, the God who is not impressed by human pretensions, because he himself is supreme over all that happens and has the power to intervene in human affairs and to change them. He is the God who specializes in overturning the present order of things, favouring the weak and the powerless, the marginalized and the poor, while bringing down the powerful and the arrogant, the rich and the complacent. In this light we are able to see that the story of David and Goliath is actually typical of the way God acts in human affairs. When this God acts, 'the bows of the mighty are broken, but the feeble gird on strength' (2:4), just as in chapter 17 God gives the victory to the insignificant shepherd lad against the powerful giant who is arrogantly confident of his victory. This is not the way people generally expect things to work out, but it should not surprise those who know this God, Israel's God, Hannah's God, the God who makes it his business to reverse the world's values and priorities. Not only David's conflict with Goliath is typical of Israel's God, but the whole story of 1 Samuel is: God favours Israel, an insignificant little nation, God favours David, an insignificant boy, and he exalts both of them: David rises to be king of Israel, and under David's rule Israel rises to become a significant power in its world.

Besides characterizing God and his actions, Hannah's song also leads us to expect that the story to follow will have something to do with a king chosen by God. Rather surprisingly, since there was no king in Hannah's own time, Hannah's song ends: The LORD 'will give strength to his king, and exalt the power of his anointed one' (2:10b). (This is Hebrew poetic parallelism: the second clause says the same thing as the first.) The statement is also surprising in view of the fact that when we read on in 1 Samuel we find that, when the people of Israel ask for a king, God does not wish to give them one. Samuel the prophet warns the people of all the evils of kingship, but they persist in demanding a king so that they may be like all the other nations. So God gives in and chooses Saul for their king (1 Sam. 8 – 10). Saul is in fact very successful in doing what the kings of other nations do for their people: he leads the people in battle against their enemies and wins victory after victory. But Saul does not please God. He turns out to be a false start for Israelite monarchy, and God chooses instead David, the man after his own heart, to make a fresh start. David is to be different, not like the kings of all the other nations. David is to redeem the very dubious institution of kingship, by ruling in the way God rules. David is not to be an oppressive, exploitative king, like the kings of all the other nations; David is to be a king who, like God, looks out for the poor and the needy, prevents exploitation, rectifies injustice. David, himself one of the poor whom God, in the words of Hannah's song, raises up from the dust, will be the anointed king who rules in solidarity with the poor, who himself raises up the poor from the dust. This is the ideal of Israelite kingship that we later find in the psalms and the prophets. It is why God chooses David and promotes his cause as the unexpected successor to King Saul.

With that background, we can enter the story in chapter 17. Israel is engaged in war with the Philistines. All through the books of Samuel Israel is fighting the Philistines, because the Philistines (from whom we get the word Palestine), who came from across the Mediterranean and invaded Palestine, settling initially on the coastal plain, were the aggressive invaders, constantly trying to expand into the areas controlled by Israel and to take over the central area of Palestine, Judaea. The battle in chapter 17 is on the frontier where the Philistines were pushing against the boundaries of Israel.

It would be easy for many modern Christian readers to be put off this story by its militaristic nature (which it shares with most of the story of David), and not to be disposed to learn anything about our relationship to God from such a passage. There is undeniably much bloodshed and slaughter in these chapters of Israel's history, wars of a kind few Christians sensitive to the values of the gospel would want to countenance today, and yet, equally undeniably, 1 Samuel portrays these as events in which God is active on the side of his people against their enemies. Two considerations may help us. One is that these chapters are not in the Bible to teach us ethics. They are not the place from which to learn about the morality of war. But, secondly, they testify to the extent of God's involvement with his chosen people Israel, chosen by God for the extraordinary task of bearing witness to the one true God before all the nations. It is part of God's humility and self-abasement for the sake of his world that God became first the God of this one, small Middle Eastern people, in order to become thereby the God of all nations. God identifies himself with this people in a period of savage conflict. It is what those times were like. God does not abstract his people from this situation, and therefore, in order to be truly with his people, God cannot abstract himself from it. These considerations may still leave us in difficulty with the text, but, once we realize that the bloodshed and the slaughter in 1 Samuel are not precedents to be followed, and that we are by no means required to approve of all that we read, we are in a position to learn from the way God deals with his people in these stories.

In chapter 17 the Israelite and Philistine camps face each other across an intervening valley. Goliath, a huge giant of a man, near seven feet tall, marches out from the Philistine encampment towards the Israelite army and bellows out a challenge. The story describes in detail how Goliath is armed, because this will be significant for David's encounter with him. He is clothed in armour from head to foot. He holds a javelin and a huge spear. A shield-bearer walks in front of him, holding up Goliath's shield in front of him so that

Goliath himself has his arms free to wield his weapons. He looks impregnable and very dangerous. His daunting challenge is for one man from the Israelite army to fight in single combat with him and for the outcome to decide the battle. He repeats the challenge every day for no less than 40 days, while nothing else happens, while the Philistines are content to let the Israelites become increasingly demoralized with every day that none of them dares rise to the challenge. Just a few more repeat performances of Goliath's dramatic act and probably the Israelites will give up.

Not only is the Israelite army thoroughly intimidated, so is their king. Saul, who has hitherto been so successful in his wars, now cowers at Goliath's challenge. He must wonder whether he should take up the challenge himself. After all, Saul himself is a big man, standing head and shoulders above most of his subjects (cf. 9:2). Should we not have expected Saul, God's anointed king, to take courage from knowing that God is with him and his army? But Saul, now deprived of God's approval, as we know from the previous chapter, no longer has confidence in God's support. In fact no one in his intimidated, dispirited army seems to think of God at all. This is a demoralized and defeatist army, with a leader who no longer has the faith or the charisma to lead or to inspire them. Only David will make a difference.

The site of the battle is only a few miles from Bethlehem, where David's family lives. Three of his brothers, the three eldest of the eight brothers, have joined the army. Presumably even brothers number four to seven were not old enough or well enough trained as soldiers to join the army, and so it goes without saying that little David, youngest of the eight, is not. But David's father sends him to the Israelite camp with some food for his brothers. This is a people's militia, in which soldiers have to supply their own provisions.

What David says when he hears about Goliath is significant: 'What shall be done for the man who kills this Philistine, and takes away the reproach from Israel? For who is this uncircumcised Philistine that he should defy the armies of the living God?' (17:26) Two concerns meet in David's mind. Certainly, he spots a possibility of bettering himself if he himself can take on Goliath successfully. The David who from this point onwards rises to power in Israel is not a man without ambition. But, in addition,

David is outraged that Goliath should be defying the armies of the living God. David is the only one who rises to Goliath's challenge because – remarkably – David is the only one who sees that God is relevant to this situation. It is revealing that he calls God 'the living God', as he will do again when he speaks to Saul (17:36). The living God is the God who is alive to act and to intervene, to enter the situation and to make a difference, the God of Hannah's song. This conviction that God is relevant is what makes David an exception in an army paralysed by fear, and it is what gives David the extraordinary idea that he may be able to defeat Goliath. He is so convinced and convincing he even, it seems, convinces Saul, though no doubt Saul by now is prepared to clutch at any straw. Obviously no one else is going to do it, so why not give the boy a chance?

What obviously demands attention in the rest of the story is the way David wins. He has neither the muscle nor the training to use the kinds of weapons Goliath wields. So, refusing Saul's offer of weapons and armour that will merely weigh him down, David uses his sling. As it turns out, this is exactly the way that Goliath can be defeated. The giant is so covered in armour and protected by his shield there is small chance of penetrating his defences without coming up close and hacking at him with a sword or thrusting a spear in, but by the time anyone got close enough to do this they would be vulnerable to Goliath's enormous strength and his own weapons. With the sling David can attack before he comes into Goliath's range and he can reach the one exposed vulnerable part of Goliath's body – his forehead. A misconception of some modern readers is that David's sling is just a boy's toy. In fact, it was a serious weapon. Back in the book of Judges, in one of the more obscure accounts of Israel at war, there is a note that the army contained 'seven hundred picked men who were left-handed; every one could sling a stone at a hair, and not miss' (Judg. 20:16). So, while David may not have learned how to fight with a sword, he was highly skilled in the use of one effective weapon, the sling. As it turned out precisely this skill was the one capable of slaying Goliath.

David's success is therefore nothing like a miracle in the ordinary sense. An atheist need find nothing inexplicable in what happens. Yet David himself unequivocally attributes it to God:

'the battle is the LORD's, and he will give you into our hand,' he yells confidently at Goliath (17:47): 'You come to me with sword and spear and javelin; but I come to you in the name of the LORD of hosts, the God of the armies of Israel, whom you have defied' (17:45). The victory is God's, not because it happens in spite of David's skill and ability, but because God prospers David's skill and ability. David is the right man in the right place at the right time. No one else, even if they were skilful with a sling, would have thought of engaging Goliath in armed combat with nothing but a sling. David, confident that God is with him, does the only thing he knows how to do, and it turns out to be the one strategy that was likely to succeed.

One lesson to be learned from this story is about genuine realism. That David of all people could take on Goliath and win seemed hopelessly unrealistic to everyone else in the Israelite camp. Saul's initial reaction to David's suggestion is the voice of realism: 'you are not able to go against this Philistine to fight with him; for you are just a boy, and he has been a warrior from his youth' (17:33). David's faith in God looks like unrealistic naivety. But once David wins, we can see that his way of fighting Goliath was actually all along the one genuinely realistic strategy for success. David's faith in God does not lead him into cloud-cuckoo-land, but actually leads him to discover the genuinely realistic possibility in the situation, which no one else has noticed. What masquerades as realism is not always the full picture. Faith may well lead us to actions that seem highly unrealistic in terms of the way people are generally viewing a situation, especially in a society that tends to err in the direction of the cynically realistic. But so-called realism can blind us to real possibilities that are genuinely there, but go unrecognized by a realism fed by fear or cynicism, or by the sort of demoralized hopelessness that infected the army of Israel and infects quite a lot of our contemporary culture. Where false realism is blind and gives up, faith and hope in God may enable us to grasp the opportunities that really can prove the way through an otherwise hopeless situation.

We can learn also from the fact that David, trusting in God, simply does what he knows he can do. From a certain point of view it might have been a bolder act of faith on David's part to wear Saul's armour and to take Saul's sword and to trust that God's miraculous power would enable him to use them. But David does not expect a miracle in that sense. He does what he knows he can do, and he trusts that God will give it success. This is often how God works. Confronted with an intimidating situation – a 'how can I possibly do anything about that?' situation – what we often need is not some unexpected ability to do things we never dreamed we could, though that sometimes happens. What we often need is the confidence that trusting in God can give us to do what we can do, little as it may seem, and to trust God to do something with that little we can do. What seems miraculous is sometimes that the thing we can do but are tempted to think could not possibly be of any real effect in such a situation turns out to be, unexpectedly, the one thing that really does make a difference to the situation. Faced with a Goliath, we have a go with the only thing we know how to use, we sling a stone, and – to everyone's amazement including our own – it is exactly the one thing that can bring Goliath down. The key is to do what we can, not letting so-called realism, cynicism or despair disarm our will to act, but trusting in God as we do what we can and leave the effects to God.

We all encounter Goliaths. Today we face some truly world-bestriding Goliaths, dominant and entrenched systems of oppressive power and corrupting influence, that intimidate all who care about truth, justice, compassion and peace. We are tempted to abandon the world to them and to cower, like the Israelites, in our Christian encampments. But we could recall David's wonderfully well-aimed slingshot and the faith that gave him the courage to make it. Even the seemingly little we can do may require considerable trust in God for it to seem worth doing. But it is what we can and therefore must do. However little it seems, we must do it as well as we can, aiming our sling as accurately as we can, and at the same time knowing that God can make of what we do much more than we can make of it ourselves. After all, these Goliaths, like the original one in David's time, are defying God, and deserve to be met with the kind of holy contempt David flung at Goliath in the name of the Lord of hosts. The same applies to the smaller Goliaths of our own particular circumstances, who may be no less intimidating to us. At them also we are authorized to shout: 'the battle is the LORD's and he will give you into our hand.'

Lord God of hosts, teach us to recognize the Goliaths that defy
you,
not to call on you to sanction our own chosen and self-seeking
causes,
but to fight only the battles you fight.
Deliver us from the paralysis of fearful acquiescence in evil
and the demoralized hopelessness that claims to be realistic.
Show us what we can do
because it is what you have given us to do.
Give us the faith to do all that we can
in the hope that you will do more than we can.

4

. . . in the stupidity born of anger

(1 Samuel 25)

In 1997 novelist Anita Diamant produced a book that met with widespread acclaim, not least from women readers. The blurb on its back cover invited bookshop browsers to 'Find out why 1.5 million women have loved this book at {www.mustread.com}', though, for those already having taken the trouble to pick the book up and read this far, another couple of minutes skimming cursorily through its opening pages would suffice to reveal the answer! The book was called *The Red Tent: The Oldest Love Story Never Told*. The following words are taken from its preface, and are set in the narrator's voice, which is also the voice of the main character in the story the book tells:

> We have been lost to each other for so long. My name means nothing to you. My memory is dust. This is not your fault, or mine. The chain connecting mother to daughter was broken, and the word passed to the keeping of men, who had no way of knowing. That is why I became a footnote, my story a brief detour between the well-known history of my father, Jacob, and the celebrated chronicle of Joseph, my brother. On those rare occasions when I was remembered, it was as a victim.

The words are directed primarily, of course, to the book's women readers (though no doubt its male readers are meant to take notice!) and decry the effective obscuring of women's stories and women characters by a tradition of storytelling dominated by men and male perspectives.

The character into whose mouth these words are put is Dinah, a woman we meet in the story told in Genesis 28 – 35. And yet, of course, it is not Dinah's story (or those of her grandmother, mother, aunts or sisters) that is told in the biblical text, but the story of her male kith and kin, a story told from a male perspective, with a clear and unflinching focus on the actions and fortunes of the male characters in it, and to which the women provide a helpful and at points invaluable backdrop. Dinah and her 'sisters' are, in E. M. Forster's terms, 'flat' rather than 'rounded' characters within this story. We learn, that is to say, little about them and are not encouraged to wonder about that which we are not told. Their narrative role is mostly incidental rather than central, though it may entail association with a single key event or idea in the plot beyond which they slip again into the shadowy background from which, fleetingly, they emerged to be noticed.[1] Dinah herself comes into just such fleeting prominence when, according to the biblical storyteller, she was 'seized' and 'defiled' or 'raped' by Shechem, the son of a local Canaanite prince. We don't know when or how the two had met, or what sort of preamble to the rape occurred. We don't know how Dinah viewed Shechem, what her perspective on the 'rape' was, how she felt about Shechem or what happened to him subsequently. We aren't told any of this because it doesn't matter from the storyteller's viewpoint. Clearly it would have mattered a great deal to Dinah, were she granted a voice. But her role in the story is effectively over within the space of a few verses. She is Jacob's daughter, the sister of Jacob's sons, and the victim of a rape. As soon as the bare 'fact' of her liaison with Shechem is established, the story becomes a male one again; the story of Shechem's desire to marry Dinah, of her father Jacob's resistance to this idea, and of the solution arrived at by two of her brothers (Simeon and Levi) to persuade Shechem and his family to undergo circumcision. And then, while they are still suffering a certain amount of post-operative discomfort, of how Jacob's sons turn up with a bunch of thugs and murder them. Politics and violence resolve the matter. It's a typically male story.

In her novel, Anita Diamant tells the same story from Dinah's point of view, and in doing so offers her readers a quite different slant on the story! It is a version of things in which Dinah is far from the simple victim, the little sister rescued gladly by her brave and noble big brothers. And it is one in which the men in the story come out with a significant amount of egg on their faces as well as blood on their swords. Whatever we may think of the novel's revisionist account of what actually happened between Dinah and Shechem, she indulges in such imaginative reconstruction precisely to provoke us, to remind us, and to protest against the fact that biblical 'history' is overwhelmingly from a male perspective, that the women characters are largely incidental props, and only very rarely show up as – to use a familiar literary category – the 'hero', the one whose wisdom or strength or love or whatever is the real point of the story and the transforming factor in the human situation of which it tells. Perhaps, Diamant is suggesting to us, this is to do less than full justice to the realities of the human past, at least if the familiar texture of the human present is anything to go by!

The Red Tent and its re-reading of Scripture are interesting when juxtaposed with our reading from 1 Samuel. In the story of David, Nabal and Abigail we have a story that in more ways than one resonates with the alternative perspective that Anita Diamant's feminist imagination urges upon us as perhaps truer to more of the biblical history than is permitted to meet the eye in the text. It is an exception that proves the rule of biblical storytelling, and in that sense strengthens rather than undermines Diamant's observation. 1 Samuel 25 is really a story about moral character, and the impact of certain sorts of human behaviour on events. We could, though, capture the essence of it further by saying that it's a story about male stupidity and female wisdom. That would be something of an overstatement – but not much of one.

The storyteller is concerned from the outset to tell us what we need to know about the husband–wife duo around whose lives this story centres. Nabal, we read in verse 3 was 'surly and mean' and, in case we need the clue, we are reminded that his name itself means 'a fool' in Hebrew. So Nabal's character is literally 'typecast' from the outset, and we can only expect the story to demonstrate the truth of the judgement encoded in his name. Meanwhile his wife, Abigail, we are told, is 'beautiful'. This, of course, is a characteristic with which we are thoroughly familiar in female characters, and which we have come almost to expect. How many 'plain' let alone physically unattractive female leads do we see in Hollywood productions? So, even though real life throws up much more aesthetic variety than the world of stories, a beautiful woman is something with which we are quite comfortable (even in Scripture), and which we expect male characters and readers alike to celebrate rather than complain about. In itself, then, female beauty is hardly something likely to subvert the ordering of male and female in our expectations, but more likely in fact to reinforce it. A beautiful woman is one whom a man – even one who is a fool – need not see as a threat to his narrative prominence, but as a welcome embellishment to his own part in the plot. But this is not all that the narrator tells us about Abigail. She's also described as 'clever', 'of good understanding' or, we might best say, wise. Indeed, as Eugene Peterson notes in his comments on this story,[2] her beauty and her wisdom are probably part and parcel of the same thing. Regardless of her physical appearance, in fact in the story it is her character first and foremost which exudes beauty and, as we shall see, duly acts as a beacon of God's own character attracting David back to a path in which it is the Lord who guides his behaviour rather than testosterone.

So, the story offers us one unambiguously stupid character, and one unambiguously good and wise character. And the good and wise character whose behaviour makes all the difference is a woman. There's the refreshing note of difference. And then we have David who is really being weighed in the balance in this story. For we are indeed still fairly early on in the story of David's relationship with the LORD here. He is only introduced into the Bible in chapter 16, where we learn quite a few things about him. He is young, brave, strong and handsome, and has been chosen by God to replace Saul as king of Israel. At this point in his story, though, he is living as an outlaw (Saul not having taken too kindly to the idea of being replaced), on the run with a band of 600 men in the wilderness. Having slaughtered Goliath, he is certainly a man with a reputation that goes ahead of him, and of which Abigail seems to have known and, unless Nabal is even more stupid than he appears to be in the story, he will have known too. David's exploits will have been the stuff of tabloid headlines – cropping up to cause havoc here and there, teasing Saul by getting so close to him as to be able to take his life, but not doing so, and then melting away again into the wilderness, eluding the best efforts of Saul's security forces to capture or kill him. It's a bit of a Robin Hood story – though David, as we shall see, is not the unambiguously good hero that legend has made Robin.

When chapter 25 opens, we find David and his men having already been in the wilderness for quite some time: hiding away from Saul; coming out to engage in skirmishes with his forces; but probably spending most of their time just 'being in the wilderness' – sitting around waiting for their next exploit; playing cards, thinking of their families, working out; whatever else it is that men do to pass the long hours on military service when there's no action. Actually, the reading suggests that they have been spending a good part of their time doing a sort of policing or peacekeeping role in the area (which recent history reminds us can be a more challenging and costly role than the military campaign itself). The wilderness is a very dangerous place – full of bandits as well as wild animals. As various stories in the Bible bear witness, just travelling through the wilderness from one settlement to the next was a risky thing to do. And those shepherds and others who were forced to spend long periods of time tending flocks out there knew only too well about the dangers. So, in verses 15-16, we read the following testimony from one of Nabal's hired shepherds (speaking of David's militia): 'The men were very good to us, and we suffered no harm, and we never missed anything when we were in the fields, as long as we were with them, they were a wall to us both by night and by day, all the while we were with them keeping the sheep.' It's the sort of testimony that many peacekeeping forces would be glad to receive from the local populace. And it seems as if Nabal's men had deliberately stayed close to David and his forces because they offered them security against the robbers and murderers who otherwise picked people off on a regular basis. And we can imagine David, perhaps, as heir apparent to the throne of this territory, and himself having been a shepherd facing just such dangers until relatively recently, being sympathetic to them and generous in his provision of protection. As our story opens, though, we actually find the shoe on the other foot. For now it is David who is the one with a need, and Nabal who is in a position to provide for that need.

Nabal, as well as being stupid and rude, is also rich and powerful. This is not a necessary conjunction in biblical terms, of course, but it is certainly one we find here. Nabal has (we are told in verse 2) 3,000 sheep and 1,000 goats. That's a lot of livestock, especially when we notice that elsewhere in Scripture Job is said to have had 7,000 sheep and 3,000 camels and, on the strength of this, to have been 'one of the most powerful men in the East' (Job 1:3). So while he certainly doesn't measure up to Job in any sense, Nabal is nonetheless a pretty wealthy and important man, and one who can afford to throw some elaborate parties. And that's what we find him doing in 1 Samuel 25. It's sheep shearing time, when all the hired men come back from the wilderness to the towns, and as well as working hard, play hard. There's feasting and celebration, letting off steam and generally enjoying being home after another hard season. And on Nabal's estate in particular, food and drink are not in short supply. In fact, as verse 36 tells us, his is a household where feasting 'fit for a king' is to be enjoyed. This turns out to be convenient (or, as it turns out for Nabal, inconvenient), because there's a king (or a king in waiting at least) nearby who wouldn't mind joining in a bit of feasting, granting his men a night on the town, and a break from the austerity rations they have been living on for months now, and of which they are all, no doubt, heartily sick.

So David, still out in the wilderness, when he hears that Nabal's place is the place to be for a party, decides that it's time to call in some favours. As we know, he has done a lot for Nabal (or for his men at least) in keeping them safe, free of charge. And he sees here the opportunity for a straightforward political quid pro quo. This, perhaps, is the first sign in the story that not all is well with David's character. Of course lots of people expect favours given to result in favours returned sooner or later. The seamy underbelly of commercial, professional and political life is full of that sort of thing, and we know it to be true of ourselves often enough in our personal relationships with others. If we do someone a favour, somewhere in the back of our mind lurks the thought that they may be in a position to return the favour one day. And there's nothing wrong with that – is there? Well, actually there may be. It certainly falls a long way short of what Jesus teaches his disciples, that good should be done to others for its own and their sake, and without a beady weather eye on the possible return; because good which is done with a view to a return is not *genuine* good at all, but a form of moral trading, and therefore a form of self-interest or selfishness. We are to do good because it's good to do good, and because the good is worth doing in and for itself. Good is good. End of story. But that's hard to put into practice, even for the one God has chosen to be king over Israel.

Here, as elsewhere in his story, David's actions show us that – with the exception of Jesus himself – biblical characters do not necessarily make healthy role models. Hungry and thirsty out in the fields, facing another cold lunch with only stream-water to drink, David's desire gets the better of him; and he sends ten of his men down into the town to greet Nabal, introduce themselves, quietly (but definitely) remind him of the gracious favour shown to his men as they watched their flocks by night, and to suggest that it might be nice for Nabal to reciprocate now by issuing an open invitation to David and his 600 well-armed friends to join the party! It's a classic case of 'I've scratched your back, you scratch mine.' Though, as it turns out, it also contains a not very well hidden 'You scratch my back, or else . . .' Again, it's a boys' thing!

From here, of course, it all goes nasty, and the foibles of both David and Nabal are given full rein. No doubt David is confident of a positive response to his 'little suggestion', and is already shaving and dressing for dinner. After all, as both he and Nabal know, he could just turn up and gatecrash if he felt like it. A couple of bouncers aren't going to be much use against a private militia. And the way David probably sees it, at least he's had the decency to ask first. But Nabal, being stupid and rude, lives up to his name and is apparently unfazed by all this. Nor is he persuaded by the suggestion that he owes David anything. Maybe he's already had a few beers by the time David's envoys arrive with the news that the future king of Israel has effectively invited himself as guest of honour to Nabal's private party.

Maybe he's a fan of Saul, and wants to make a sharp political point. Or maybe he is just, as his name says, stupid. Whatever; his ill-mannered, ill-judged response is designed deliberately to provoke:

> David who? And who do you think you are, showing up with demands from someone I don't know, have never met, and whose only credentials are that the King's secret police are trying to track him down. Why on earth should I waste my hard earned cash on pampering fugitives? I'm an important man in this town you know; I can't be compromising my reputation by being associated with troublemakers. It'd be all over the local paper and I'd be ruined. I might even have my Rotary membership revoked . . .

That, at least, is the gist of his response. It's not the most intelligent response in the world, given David's reputation and Nabal's relative lack of military muscle. But it fits his character as a fool.

'So', we read, 'David's men turned away, and came back, and told him all this' (verse 12). And . . . what? Wouldn't that be a great point at which to end an episode if this were a serial? What will David say now? How will he in his turn respond to this raising of the political stakes? Well, we discover in verse 13 that David, too, is a typical male, seemingly determined to solve any and every problem in life by resorting to violence (and in this case violence of a wholly disproportionate sort). 'He said to his men "Every man strap on his sword!" Every one of them strapped on his sword; and David also strapped on his sword; and about four hundred men went up after David.' And on the journey David burns with anger at the insult Nabal has delivered, and already savours the taste of the anticipated revenge: 'It was obviously a waste of time protecting this man in the wilderness. He has returned me evil for good. Okay, so be it. Now he'll see what people get when they snub David. God do so to David and more also, if by tomorrow morning there's a single man left alive in Nabal's household.'

And so, at last, as David and his band of peacekeepers-turned-dubious-vigilantes appear over the horizon, we meet again Abigail, Nabal's wife, warned by servants of her husband's immodest and ill-judged outburst, and shrewd enough to realize that, men being men, this whole situation is likely to end in the horror and futility of violence. Abigail takes it upon herself in effect to act in her husband's place, substituting her own strategy of moral and political persuasion for the strong-headed, rash and ill-advised refusal to compromise that is all he knows. She opts to do what, had he had any sense, Nabal himself would have done from the outset – bite his lip, quell any justifiable sense of annoyance he might have felt at being taken for granted or exploited, and offered the hospitality sought by David and his men. So, in order both to undo the damage already done and to avert any worsening of the situation, Abigail prepares a meal – a concrete gesture of the generosity of which her words and gestures will duly speak – loads it onto two donkeys, and sets off with it to intercept David's army before it reaches Nabal's estate. Because Abigail recognizes that if David ever crosses the boundaries of the estate, then, whatever she attempts, it will be impossible to isolate Nabal for long enough to do what must be done. He will be bound to hear of David's approach and, even in his drunkenness, come out, his anger inflamed now by a toxic mixture of the wine, the sight of David's men on his land, and the humiliation of his wife attempting to usurp his prerogative as head of the household. So, if she's to act as mediator between the two parties and avoid the otherwise inevitable bloodshed and loss of life, it's vital that Abigail catches David still on the march, in the wilderness, on neutral territory, and intercedes with him there, diverting him in one way or another from his determination to teach Nabal a lesson he won't forget.

The episode that follows reveals Abigail, in fact, to be the unexpected hero and the victor of the story. She is the one who shows genuine strength, and who finally overcomes and triumphs. But her victory and strength, of course, are of a moral rather than a military sort, and they result not in the obliteration of the one who confronts her, but in his transformation. Abigail triumphs, paradoxically, by assuming a position of abject humility and weakness before the approaching threat. She gets down off her donkey as David and his well-oiled and powerful military machine approaches, and kneels down in the road before him, forcing him to a halt. For many readers, the image will resonate with memories of TV coverage of the incident in Beijing's

Tiananmen Square in 1989 when Chinese students opposed a heavily armoured military force deployed by politicians to disperse their protest, defying the tanks with nothing more than their own fragile flesh and blood. It was a remarkable stand-off, producing a moment of incredible drama, tension and expectation. What would the soldiers do? It was clear enough where all the power lay. Would they really roll on regardless, crushing the protest both metaphorically and literally? Or would the pathetic vulnerability of their opponents and the ridiculous disproportion of military advantage and disadvantage in the circumstance jar them out of the cocoon which their training had deliberately induced, jolt their sense of perspective, revealing the common humanity shared with those who dared block their path in this way and awakening them to the moral realities of their situation? We would be naive to suppose that, human nature being what we know it to be and to be capable of, there was ever any guarantee for those who blocked the tanks' path with nothing more than their bodies. Yet nor was it a completely desperate and arbitrary gesture. All the military might lay with the tanks; but the human strength lay elsewhere, and everyone knew it.

Like those protesters, Abigail in our story shows both remarkable courage and a depth of human wisdom. To allow Nabal to meet David's military might with his own would inevitably lead to a contest ending with the hollow 'victory' of the physically superior over the physically weak. To confront him with a show of vulnerability, fragility, weakness and generous goodness, though, confronts him with a striking moral dilemma and thereby robs him of the advantage he otherwise holds. He cannot march straight over Abigail (a woman, of all things!) without at least losing a massive amount of public good will, something that no ambitious political figure can easily afford. In any case, Abigail suspects that David is not the sort of monster who would ever do such a thing; he is a man who has allowed himself to be drawn into the sort of futile escalation of military stakes that is so easy to join in the heat of anger, but hard to escape from subsequently without significant loss of face – something else that hails political disaster. Abigail gives him a mutually convenient way out. She presents him with a circumstance in which he can call his raiding party to a halt while yet retaining his dignity (a dignity that her disposition of obeisance holds secure). And, once she has his ear, her carefully chosen words effectively exorcize the demon of militaristic machismo that held him temporarily in its thrall, and show him just how what he was planning to do would look when viewed in the cold light of day or, more to the point, from a God's-eye point of view:

> Upon me alone, my lord, be the guilt; . . . don't even take my husband seriously. He's a fool as his name alone declares, and he's really not worth the trouble that violence now will cause. Do you really want to waste your energy on him? And just stop and think – how is this going to look when you have demonstrated your military superiority? Is it going to be seen to have been worthwhile, justified, the sort of thing a King of Israel should get mixed up in? The LORD will deal with your enemies. Leave vengeance to him in his infinite justice. Now – accept this gift of food and drink for your men (if only they had come to me in the first place instead of going to that idiot Nabal!), and depart in peace, with no harm done. Forgive my husband his stupidity – he really can't help it, and it's nothing personal.

David is shaken by this speech out of his rage and his baser instincts, and realizes the folly of his own reaction to Nabal. He grants Abigail's request, calls back the troops before they have engaged in battle, and – remarkably – thanks her for the wisdom she has shown in speaking truth into a situation otherwise driven on by a frenzy of prejudice, injustice and foolishness. He passes the test; but that he does so is not thanks to himself alone. It is Abigail's wisdom, her heroic willingness to put herself in the way of David's fury and to presume to question his actions, which saves him from himself,

In a radio discussion of the 2003 war in Iraq one contributor suggested it was a pity that women rather than men had not been responsible for the international negotiations that preceded and led up to it. Women, it was indicated, do not see violence or force as the most obvious resort in situations of conflict. It's an interesting if a contentious suggestion, and one made, unsurprisingly, by a woman commentator! This story, though, inadvertently reinforces its suggestion. For in it, it is indeed – as it happens – female wisdom that prevails over masculine foolishness, and thereby saves David from the 'bloodguilt' that might have disqualified him from becoming Israel's king. Crushing anyone who proved inconvenient with military superiority (no matter how insignificant a threat they might in reality present to his own security) was, after all, the very strategy Saul had adopted, and God had duly rejected as appropriate for one who would rule over his chosen people. It's interesting to speculate whether the story of David and Abigail also has its provenance in a tradition passed on by women rather than men! But putting Abigail on a pedestal would be the very last thing the writer – whether male or female – will have been interested in doing. Biblical stories are not finally much concerned with human heroes or heroines, but with God and his dealings with us. And it is God who is the one acting behind the scenes here, who, as Abigail and David both acknowledge, has sent Abigail as his agent to test David's moral mettle, and to be the bringer of God's own peace in place of the violence and destruction to which David had been so looking forward.

But the story does make the point (all too easy to forget if we allow the general tenor of biblical narration to shape our thinking) that when the chips are down, the God of Scripture can and does choose and use female wisdom and beauty of character as an instrument in shaping his purposes in history. Maybe, if truth be known, he is driven to do so on a much more regular basis than meets the eye!

> Stay our hand, Lord,
> when it does stupidity's bidding,
> bring to nothing the evil and cruelty
> conceived in the heat of misplaced passion.
> May wisdom's beauty stop us in our tracks
> and turn us again into the narrow way
> of your kingdom.
> Amen.

. . . in the clutches of sin

(2 Samuel 11)

The story of David, Uriah and Bathsheba has to rank among the most gripping for readers ancient and modern alike. It has all the key ingredients: sex, power, corruption, death; and it is told with skill, in a way that raises the level of tension gradually as the plot unfolds, keeping us on the edges of our seats to the bitter end. Its heady mixture of classic love-triangle, royal scandal, murder and tragic cot death rivals the best and the worst of soap opera plots and Sunday newspaper exclusives in terms of so-called human interest. Yet the writer's vision is deeper, and takes us further into the joys and griefs of the human condition than the media hack is capable of doing. This story shows us something of what it means to live in fellowship with David's God and our God, and the often uncomfortable consequences of doing so.

Part of what makes a story a good story is its fusion of things that are and things that are not true of its readers. It is precisely because stories relate us to something that is recognizably our world and ourselves that they are able, by showing us at the same time something unfamiliar and mysterious, to change our way of seeing and experiencing this same world, and thereby to change us. When the book is placed back down on the bedside table (or wherever) and the vision fades, we find that we have a slightly different perspective on things, that we have learned something not just about some other (real or imaginary) time, place and character, but about *ourselves* in the process.

That, surely, is true in *this* story in which the familiar pattern of temptation, fall, guilt, punishment and restoration is opened up for us imaginatively in ways lying beyond the range of the most informative or theologically astute of lectures or sermons on sin. Through immersion in the story we indwell the messy complexity of sin and its consequences; we feel its discomfort, we identify it as a place that we, in our own way, have visited many times, sometimes willingly. And yet, because of the detachment which storytelling permits (we are not David – we *watch* him from the relative comfort of our place beyond the page) we are able to see the situation from several different angles at once. Part of us is with David, understanding the impulses and urges that drive him on, 'knowing' exactly why he does what he does, and wondering whether – in his shoes – we should have the strength to do anything different. Another part of us is able to observe the pattern of events and see where it is all headed (unlike David we have the luxury, if we choose to avail ourselves of it, of skipping a couple of pages to check), and able to feel the outrage any decent person would feel.

This, then, is a powerful story that engages and shapes our moral sensibilities. As one commentator puts it (nicely): 'The writer has cut very, very deep into the strange web of foolishness, fear and fidelity that comprises the human map. This narrative is more than we want to know about David, and more than we can bear to understand about ourselves.' Like all stories, this one comes with some components fitted as standard. It has a narrative context. It fits, that is to say, into a bigger story of which it is part, and we approach it already knowing some important things about its central character. It has some central action or event, something that is done by or happens to the character whose story it is. And it has an outcome or outcomes that may be more or less predictable depending on the sort of story it is. These are the things that draw us in and keep us reading, and we may as well treat them in turn.

As readers we are first introduced to David in 1 Samuel 16, and readers of the intervening 26 chapters, observing his rise from shepherd boy to become the most powerful man in Israel, have had opportunity in plenty to gauge his character. Such rapid and dramatic changes of fortune are generally very revealing, drawing the best or the worst out of a person. By now, therefore, we are confident that we know just what sort of man David is, and the judgement is solidly – if not unambiguously – positive. Let's reflect on some of its finer points.

David is loyal. The Old Testament has a word that it uses chiefly of God to indicate God's faithfulness to Israel – *hesed*. God keeps his promises, is utterly reliable, can be trusted, especially in a crisis. And David, we might say, mirrors God's character in this respect. He too is *hesed*, faithful; to his friends, to his enemies, to God, to God's covenant, to God's people. In this, as in other ways, he proves to be the ideal ruler for Israel, because in his dealings with the nation he is a flesh-and-blood parable of Israel's one true King – God himself (see 1 Sam. 8:7). Again, like his God, David is also merciful and just in his exercise of enormous power. There is no hint of oppression or sleaze in his career. In what is every tabloid columnist's worst nightmare, David turns out to be a political leader of integrity and principle with no skeletons rattling in his cupboard. His reign is one in which the law-breaker may be sure of justice being righteously administered, and the weak and disadvantaged confident of whatever protection and assistance the government is able to afford. David is also prayerful, a fact to which the preceding may, perhaps, in no small part be ascribed. He frequently 'inquires of the Lord' before making or executing policy. And David is clear and mindful from the outset of his 40-year reign that it is God who has *established* him as king, and that he has done so not for *David's* sake but 'for the sake of his people' (2 Sam. 5:12). Not surprisingly, therefore, David is both successful and popular. In both foreign and domestic policy his leadership flourishes, and with it the nation. A period of peace and prosperity has dawned in Israel's life, with all the benefits of monarchy and few if any of the attendant disadvantages (see 1 Sam. 8:10-22). It presented, we may suppose, quite a contrast to the model of kingly rule more familiar among Israel's neighbours, and duly became the basis for Israel's imagining of how God's own coming kingdom would be (see, for example, the vision of the reign of 'the stock of Jesse' in Isaiah 11).

Faithful; reliable; righteous; merciful; prayerful; successful; popular: this, then, is the David about whom we now read in 2 Samuel 11. Or is it? From the very outset of the passage before us, a quite different note is struck in the portrayal of David's character. A note which suggests that the power and success that David enjoys have finally skewed his vision, and have become detached from those virtues that made him the great king he has undoubtedly been. In this new episode in the soap opera of David's life a shift is effected from public triumph and acclaim to personal pathos; from a life under blessing to a life under curse. And it is sin, of course, which gets a stranglehold and spoils everything. Sin, this story reminds us – even a 'quick fling' with no strings attached – cuts deep into the moral fabric of God's world, and may have consequences that extend way beyond the immediate aftermath of the deed itself.

'But David remained at Jerusalem' (11:1). As our story opens, David is already cast in a dubious light as a leader who nowadays prefers to lead from the rear rather than the front, allowing others to do his dirty and dangerous work for him. It is, the narrator advises us, springtime, the time when kings (we can almost hear the ironic gloss, '*real* kings . . .') go out to battle. No longer the bold warrior king who faces and defeats even the most daunting of Israel's enemies (compare 1 Sam. 8:20 with 1 Sam. 17:41-54), these days David lets others put themselves at risk in his stead while he remains at home in safety and takes advantage of their absence.

The advantage David 'takes' on this occasion is a woman who inadvertently becomes the object of his desire. From his rooftop vantage point he discovers that he has an inconveniently direct view of a neighbouring bathroom where this woman is, well, bathing! David indulges in a little aroused voyeurism, and his imagination is quickly hooked by her beauty. She is defined for us from the outset as the wife of another man, a man who is away at the battle (where David himself ought to be). But, being the king, David is able to convert sinful fantasy into even more sinful reality without too much difficulty. He sees the woman, wants her and takes her (see vv. 3-4). There is no complex process of moral reasoning. He is *king* after all! He is in control. He sends men to their deaths in battle, and summons women to his bedroom for his own personal satisfaction. No romance, no wooing, just lust and its clumsy physical gratification. He 'takes' her. Then she returns home. No flowers, no nice meal, no will she/won't she?

He takes her. We aren't told whether she is complicit, flattered, afraid, . . . and frankly it's not really relevant. She has no choice in the matter. She is not a person but an object. The verb 'takes' says it all.

This, then, is a rather different David. A David who takes what he wants, simply because – he realizes – he *can*. It's a dangerous and destructive discovery. What even David cannot control, though, is the biological outcome of his adultery. The woman discovers she is pregnant. Bathsheba's first words in the story are ones that rob David of his control: 'I'm pregnant'. David is neither the first nor the last political leader to have his comfortable and self-fulfilling lifestyle thrown into turmoil by these two words. The threat to his reputation must be apparent at once. His secret sin is about to become very public unless some drastic action is taken. With all the men of sexually active age, including Bathsheba's husband, away at the war, and with David's penthouse suite overlooking Bathsheba's bathroom, conclusions would quickly enough be drawn. It could all add up to a public relations disaster and a plunge in the monarchy's popularity stakes.

Of course, sexual sin is actually the least of it, though it may be what attracts most attention in our own sexually obsessed age. It's bad enough. But the main focus of David's faithlessness to God and to his people lies elsewhere, in the exploitation of the vulnerable, the abuse of his God-given position of power, the abrogation of his duty to be God's representative in Israel's midst. It is *here* that the real misdemeanour lies. And it is this that threatens to do irreparable damage to David's relationship with his people. For David to enter into an adulterous affair, or even have a one-night stand, with another man's wife, is no small matter and we should not trivialize it. But nor should our own society's chosen preoccupation with sex obscure the more significant moral fault. This is not just sex. It is sex to order; sex without consideration for the other; sex as self-gratification; sex which David enjoys not just without thought for Bathsheba's well-being (no doubt he has it in mind to repay her with some suitable 'gift'), but without thought for its effect on her relationship with her husband who is at this very moment laying his own life on the line, fighting David's battles for him. Yes, David should have kept his trousers on. But sex here is only the occasion for a darker deed. David's behaviour is essentially a betrayal. It is a betrayal of the God who has called him and given him so much. And it is a betrayal of the people who have invested so much trust in him. The seductive allure of a moment is transformed by action into a royal abuse of trust and privilege. Now, we might suppose, is the time for some serious penitence and facing of the consequences? Maybe there's still time to turn this around? But in the story things get worse rather than better.

One impulsive and damaging action is followed quickly by another in this man's slide down the moral slope. With little apparent compunction, David acts quickly in defence of his own interests. He calls Uriah back from the battle lines and attempts to orchestrate a different, more acceptable explanation for Bathsheba's pregnancy. Once the baby begins to show, it will be remembered by all how Uriah was indeed back fleetingly in Jerusalem around the time that conception would have occurred. It's the perfect cover up! But for it to work, of course, Uriah must actually play his part in the drama. So David, having debriefed Uriah about the campaign, grants him leave to go home, and actually urges him, with the sort of coarse euphemism that passes between men in the locker room, to make the most of his visit. 'Go down to your house', he tells him, and 'wash your feet'! David might reasonably have supposed that he could rely on Uriah's natural desire for his wife, combined with the fact that any opportunity granted him now to see her might never come again, since he was returning to a battle in which his life could so easily be lost. Uriah would get something he wanted, Bathsheba would be glad enough to see her husband (and, if she knew what was good for her, keep quiet), and David would be let off the hook. It was a win-win-win situation.

But what David did not account for was the moral complexity of Uriah. And here the storyteller's art is at its most skilful. For Uriah, although he has both the right and the opportunity to be with his wife that night, chooses not to. Why? Well, as he tells David the following morning, he feels uncomfortable taking advantage of this unlooked-for blessing when his friends and neighbours, all that he holds dear apart from his family, are at risk in the field of battle. Out of loyalty and sense of solidarity with his fellow combatants, Uriah will not enjoy the comfort and pleasure of the marriage bed. And this, of course, sets him in direct contrast to David himself, the man who should have been on the battlefield leading his men and wasn't; the man who had no right, but created his own opportunity to defile Uriah's marriage by taking his wife into his own bed for pleasure's sake alone. The moral irony is pronounced, and can hardly be lost on David. And so, once again, for all his royal power, David cannot control everything: and he is driven to still more desperate measures in order to cover his tracks.

If Uriah will not do the one thing David thinks he can rely on, then Uriah must be disposed of. But this time David's alibi must be rock solid. So, after spending an evening *drinking* with the man whose death he is plotting, David contacts Joab and arranges for Uriah to be returned not just to the battle but to its most treacherous part, rendering Uriah's heroic death all but certain. In fact Joab sends many of his men into wholly unacceptable danger in order to secure this single desired outcome. The cynicism of the entire episode is breathtaking. Uriah, a foreigner in Israel's midst (he is a Hittite not an Israelite) shows himself to be a faithful servant of David and thereby of God, even unto death. David, on the other hand, who, as King of Israel is supposed to protect and to serve his people within the covenant, shows himself to be capable of an utterly exploitative series of actions in which power becomes a means to self-protection and self-serving at the expense of the other. It's the very opposite of all that David is supposed to be and to do. First, Bathsheba and then Uriah are drawn into the circle of this abuse, and not just as individuals. In their vulnerability they are surely representative of Israel as a whole: a people which loves and trusts its king, and is being taken for a fool in what happens here, as David seeks, just for a while, to be an absolute monarch, and to set himself above the law. From the guilt, fear and anxiety which one sin generates in David's spirit, many more and worse things follow quickly on.

What we see here is how sin is never an isolated, purely individual affair. It sends out ripples and waves of disturbance and pain in all directions; and the consequences run on and on. No doubt David had realized as soon as Bathsheba departed his bed that what he had just done with her could have some unfortunate outcomes, quite apart from being wrong in itself. But he surely never envisaged having to deceive and scheme and sink to the depths that he sinks to here in a bid to draw a line under the whole sorry affair. In any case, while moral utilitarianism may have something to be said for it as a theory, at the point of temptation we have remarkable capacities for self-delusion, and the intense pleasures of the anticipated moment can seem to weigh far more heavily than even the longest chain of unfortunate events that may or may not follow from indulging it. But sin is organic. It infects the wound it causes in the moral fabric of our lives with others, and the infection spreads all too rapidly.

Having indulged in some very seedy power games in order to stop the rot, to protect his profile and his popular influence, David presumably thinks he can now sit back and breathe easily again. With Uriah dead, he takes Bathsheba as his own wife. The child born to her can now be owned as his with impunity, and she at least will be protected from all too familiar economic and social consequences of being widowed. It's hardly heart-warming charity, and it is a dreadful moral mess, but in some sense David is here taking a degree of responsibility for things.

But now, of course, we see David's other great miscalculation. Just as he discovers that he can't control Bathsheba's biology, and can't presume upon Uriah's capitulation to desire, so he duly realizes that he has entirely overlooked the all-seeing eye of the God to whom he used to be so close, and in whose service his life is supposed to be spent. What on earth was David thinking of, covering up his misdemeanour from human gaze, and at terrible cost to others, when all the time the one person whose judgement really mattered or counted for anything was able to see not just the outward course of events, but the inner motivations behind David's actions? Because God, like those who hear the story narrated, can see inside David's head and heart, knows David, in fact, better than David knows himself. But David has forgotten the LORD. God no longer forms part of the moral calculus in accordance with which he frames his behaviour. In fact, tellingly, God's name has not been mentioned once in this whole sorry story so far, having last been heard on David's lips in 2 Samuel 9:3 where, he asks one of his courtiers, 'is there anyone left of the house of Saul to whom I may show the kindness (*hesed*) of God?'.

The 'kindness' or 'loyalty' or 'faithfulness' of God! The question drips with irony when read in the light of David's actions in chapter 11. 'People to whom I may show the kindness of God.' When David asked this question he still knew what his calling was. He still saw God at work in every event, and saw God's purpose for him having implications in every circumstance. But now God has dropped out of the picture entirely. That tends to happen when we know we are deliberately doing something that God hates us to do. It's too hard to do it under his gaze, so we airbrush him out. David has done precisely this: but God hasn't gone away. As the silent, secret character in the story he has seen and heard everything, and now he has some urgent business to do with David, his chosen king, the one into whose hands he had entrusted the well-being of his people.

The story of the prophet Nathan and his parable is really a story in its own right, skilfully told, and with its own set of tensions and resolutions and eventual punch-line. But it also serves as the dramatic climax to this unhappy episode in David's story.

Notice first how although David knows he has done wrong, he does not yet have it in proper perspective. And so the parable, engaging his own strong and well-formed sense of morality, generates a suitably ironic exchange. Like Nathan, we can see precisely what is happening. We don't need to be told '*You* are the man'. We can already see the moral parallelism between the actions of the 'rich man' in the parable and David's own behaviour. But David does not see it: not *yet* anyway. So, when the story is told, David's outrage is considerable, even to the point where his kingly prerogative as judge kicks in automatically and (notice!!) *God's* name suddenly returns to his lips as relevant: 'As the Lord lives, the man who has done this deserves to die . . . he shall restore the lamb fourfold, because he *did* this thing, and because he had *no pity*.' It's not just the theft which David so abhors: it is the clear abuse of power and privilege, and the complete lack of consideration for the poor and disadvantaged (who in God's eyes are deserving of special protection and care as prescribed in the law). Here, then, is another level of irony. David guilelessly adopts God's perspective, as he is called to do as judge, and condemns the man in Nathan's story. Yet it is a perspective to which he has blinded himself in his own life. And then comes the punch-line: 'You are the man!' *You* David. You did this. This is your story, and not one from which you are comfortably detached. Take a reality check. *You* have become an abuser of the vulnerable ones placed in your care. His imagination tantalized by Nathan's skilful storytelling, David has been drawn in hook, line and sinker, and is now held firm, wriggling uncomfortably on the end of his own accusation (which is also God's accusation).

And so, at last, God addresses David through his prophet: 'David – why have you *done* this? I gave you *everything*. You never lacked *anything*. I placed power, land, riches, happiness all within your grasp. And I would have given more if you had asked. So *why*? Why betray me, break my trust, and abuse your people? Why?' They are words of anguish and deep disappointment; the sort of words we might expect from a father chastening a son or daughter in parallel circumstances. But, of course, they are also words of judgement: and God goes on to describe the way David's actions will devastate the comfortable life he has hitherto enjoyed, skewing his relationships, forcing him to live with guilt and shame, and family breakdown. The moral consequences of David's evil cannot be shirked or covered up. He has to own them and to face them. They are, after all, his due; the 'wages' of his sin.

Far from continuing with the pretence, or seeking to justify himself, David quietly concurs with what he now knows to be true. 'I have sinned against the Lord.' You *could* say, 'well, there's not much *point* arguing with God', and that would be true enough. But David's response expresses much more than this. Here, as so often elsewhere in the Bible, God's judgement comes as a healing and redemptive force in someone's life. It is painful. But the pain is that which engenders transformation. Whatever has gotten into David in these few chapters, whatever madness has beset him or seized him with its influence, has blinded him to the reality of his circumstance, and prevented him from seeing the moral realities of things. He knows he is not doing right; but that is a far cry from realizing the frightening dimensions of the wrong he is committing. Not that there is ever any suggestion here that David is anything but responsible for his actions. He is, and now he must bear their awful cost. But in restoring him, forgiving him and punishing him, the LORD also *redeems* him by realigning his distorted vision of things, and enabling him to see himself and his circumstance as others are seeing them. Nathan's parable achieves what accusation and argument alone could never have achieved. David, sinful and guilty, is restored to his right mind, seeing the world again through eyes that are attuned to God's own.

What, then, may we take from this story? Can we find *ourselves* in it, and if so where? No doubt the answers will be different for each of us at different points in our lives. The most natural thing is probably for us to seek some identification with the central character of David, and doubtless we should. No matter what our roles and responsibilities in life, susceptibility to the allure of sex or power is shed around generously, and is likely to tempt us at some stage in some form. What this story makes clear is the potential snowball effect of what may seem at first to be a small and insignificant indiscretion. Sin leads to more sin. What begins as an isolated matter quickly grows and smothers us, gathering us up in a downward rush, which leads, sooner or later, to death and destruction. Maybe there is a particular point about the responsibilities and challenges attaching to leadership, or to those whose walk is especially close to God. When sin gets a hold and begins to wreak havoc here, the impact is so much more spectacular and significant. We should also be prepared, though, to find ourselves in other characters and their experience. There may well be times when we are in danger of becoming a Bathsheba, or are called to be a Nathan. The church probably needs more Nathans. Because if sin needs to be stopped early, before it gets a hold, then we need to recognize it, face up to it and be honest about it with one another. And sometimes, in order for that to happen, we *need* the painful process of having our image reflected back to us: we need to see ourselves as others see us, to be shaken out of the cocoon of self-deceit and self-justification which we so readily surround ourselves with. Before it all gets horribly out of hand.

> Out of my soul's depth to thee my cries have sounded;
> Let thine ears my plaints receive, on just fear grounded.
> Lord, shouldst thou weigh our faults, who's not confounded?

But with grace thou censur'st thine when they have erred,
Therefore shall thy blessed name be lov'd and feared.
Ev'n to thy throne my thoughts and eyes are reared.

Thee alone my hopes attend, on thee relying;
In thy sacred word I'll trust, to thee fast flying,
Long ere the watch shall break, the morn descrying.

In the mercies of our God who live secured,
May of full redemption rest in him assured,
Their sin-sick souls by him shall be recured.[1]

. . . in the pride born of influence

(2 Kings 5:1-14)

When we first meet him in this story, Naaman is to all appearances a man with every reason to be content. He already has most of the things that many people in our day spend a lot of time and effort striving for in life. As commander of the military forces of Aram (the territory which bordered Israel to the north, where modern-day Syria is) Naaman would no doubt have been wealthy, in a position of considerable influence (he was, we are told in verse 1, 'in high favour' with the king), highly successful in his career (a 'mighty warrior', who had delivered victory over Israel on the battlefield to his king) and on the rapid track to an early retirement with a very attractive pension arrangement. What more could a man possibly want? But the story reminds us, as the Bible so often does, that such material success alone cannot supply real contentment. And Naaman, for all his power and influence, suffers from a disfiguring, humiliating, socially ruinous (because contagious) and seemingly incurable skin disease whose ironic advance on his body marches relentlessly on as the days pass. That's Naaman's paradox: one of the most successful and powerful men alive, he is yet utterly vulnerable and powerless to redeem himself from this assault on his own flesh.

We may take it that a man in Naaman's position would already have consulted the best private doctors in Damascus, and perhaps even tried a few of the alternative remedies that could be purchased from furtive-looking 'sales executives' in the bazaar. By the time we catch up with him it seems that he has already reached desperation point. It's not easy to disguise leprosy, once its ravages spread to those parts of the body that are difficult to cover up in normal everyday life. And Naaman's problem has become so apparent that even the servants in his household are talking about it (though no doubt behind his back rather than to his increasingly disfigured face).

The domestic gossip eventually reaches the ears of Naaman's wife's maid – as it happens, an Israelite girl taken captive on one of Naaman's own raiding parties across the border. This marks a significant change in Naaman's fortunes. For the girl remembers hearing stories about a man of God in Samaria, a prophet with a reputation for doing amazing things in the power of God's Spirit, and someone who, she is convinced, could easily cure a man of leprosy.

Despite her anonymity, and precisely because of her apparent misfortune as a recently acquired piece of military 'booty', this young girl plays a vital role in the story simply by bearing witness to what she knows. She tells her mistress about the prophet. It's a 'bit' part in the drama, but one without which it could not unfold as it does. Viewed from the perspective of what follows, we can see this 'girl from the land of Israel' as God's spokeswoman – in the right place at the right time, and glad to tell of the good things which the religion of her birth affords to those who will avail themselves of it. That's it. She can – and need – do nothing more. Her part in the story is closed, and we hear no more of her beyond it. This bit of intimate female chit-chat, though, is not to remain long in the privacy of the dressing room, but feeds uncomfortably into the already complicated and demanding mixture of Naaman's life.

So – perhaps at dinner that same evening – Naaman's wife tells Naaman ('Do you know, my maid said the oddest thing this afternoon . . .'); and Naaman – well, how should we imagine him reacting? Even if he takes the girl's claims seriously, what exactly is he to do? He's one of the most powerful and respected men in Aram, but that probably makes him someone feared and perhaps even hated in Israel. Aram is effectively at war with Israel and, even though Aram has Israel in a military stranglehold, Naaman is hardly likely to be welcomed with open arms there, let alone given the red carpet treatment if he shows up asking for a medical favour. And then there's the whole humiliation thing. There are lengths to which a man can reasonably be expected to go to sort out his problems: but visiting the shaman of a foreign religion, and probably being put through God alone knows what mumbo-jumbo ceremony, with smoke, and unguents, and chanting . . . It's enough to make your skin creep. But then, Naaman's skin is already creeping, and if there's any chance that this could actually work, maybe it's just worth a try.

So, Naaman sets off, with a letter of introduction from his king, to visit the court of Israel in Samaria, this time on a 'social' visit. He sets off with his regular train of camels and chariots and troops, and on this occasion a considerable chunk of the Aramean gross national product, because Israel hadn't yet discovered the benefits of a national health service, and Naaman could certainly afford to go private. And he goes, as all reasonable assumptions demand that he should, to the centre of Israel's political and military power – to the king's palace. Surely, if there is a man in Israel powerful enough to cure someone of leprosy, then this is where he will be found? And so we get the marvellous moment in the story where Naaman's personal problem almost sparks off an international incident! Jehoram, the King of Israel, sees Naaman marching up to the palace with his retinue, and then reads the letter that he has brought with him; and he can only see it as a cynical ploy to start another fight. 'Here's my man Naaman. He has leprosy. You cure him of it. Or else . . .' Jehoram's incredulity quotient is set pretty low. To be fair, though, as readers of Christian Scripture we need to remind ourselves that he hasn't had his sense of the bizarre dulled by regular reading of Gospel stories about Jesus healing lepers, and his response is more in tune with what might reasonably be taken for common sense: 'What do you mean, cure him of leprosy. Who do think I am? God?' And things are just starting to get very uncomfortable in the negotiations (Jehoram is pretty sure this can probably be construed as failing to meet some United Nations resolution or other, and suspects that Naaman has tanks waiting on the border, just itching for an excuse to use them) when Elisha, the prophet, hears of the situation, and sends a message to the king. 'Don't panic. Send Naaman to me, and let me deal with him, that he may learn that there is a prophet in Israel' (verse 8).

And so we come to the penultimate, humorous scene, with Naaman's chariots and soldiers and camels all piling up outside Elisha's house. And, as the dust settles, Naaman climbs down from his chariot and walks up the garden path to the door, maybe having the heat of the day fanned away from him by two servants with large feather air conditioning units as he goes. And, as the door opens, Naaman steels himself to meet this religious witch doctor, maybe all the more apprehensive now that he finds himself out of the familiar surroundings of government, and forced to track someone down in a backstreet clinic.

But Elisha doesn't even come to the door. He sends a messenger, who tells Naaman: 'Thanks for coming. Elisha's actually a bit busy just now; but he says, just call in at the Jordan on your way home and dip yourself in seven times. The problem should clear up within a couple of days'. It's a classic 'put-down' line, and ratchets the level of tension in the story up from frenetic to breaking point! And, of course, the story is really all about this moment – how will Naaman react? Has Elisha just seriously reduced the odds of a happy ending, and trebled the premiums on his personal life-assurance policy? Will this demonstration of prophetic indifference to this-worldly power and influence finally push Naaman over the edge, and result in a temper tantrum with apocalyptic consequences? Will many more young Jewish girls suddenly find themselves facing unexpected career opportunities in the kitchens and boudoirs of Syria's well-to-do? Everything builds up to this moment, and everything hinges on it. It's a test of Naaman's character, by God.

Initially it looks as though it's a test he's going to fail, albeit not in the frenzy of bloodshed which Hollywood scriptwriters might prefer for the film version. 'Naaman', we read, 'became angry, and went away, saying "I thought that for me he would surely come out, and stand and call on the name of the LORD his God, and would wave his hand over the spot, and cure the leprosy! Are not Abana and Pharpar, the rivers of Damascus, better than all the waters of Israel? Could I not wash in them and be clean?" He turned and went away in a rage' (verses 11-12). It's a complex response. At one level of course it is the reaction of pure pique and sense of having been suborned. This is not how he is used to being treated by people, let alone backstreet religious fanatics without even a significant political office to back them up. Just coming to this neighbourhood has been a bit of a come-down, given the professional and social circles that Naaman normally moves in; and now this supposedly great man of God won't even show his face, but sends a menial out to speak on his behalf. It's outrageous behaviour, and makes Naaman look foolish in the eyes of his men. But there's another aspect to his reaction too. It's one of disillusion and disappointment. Having come all this way, having taken the risk of yet another promised remedy falling flat, Naaman at least wants to feel that the journey was worth the effort; and he was expecting to be subjected to a bona fide religious ritual for his troubles. But Elisha refuses to pander to these expectations. No hype. No ritual or ceremony. No dramatic invocation of divine power with smoke and bells and whistles. Just 'go and bathe in the Jordan on your way home'. Surely Elisha is pulling his leg? This isn't part of the scenario he had agreed to let himself in for. It's all a con, as well as a humiliation. If he'd wanted to try the healing powers of river water, then Aram had two perfectly good rivers of its own, thank you very much. So Naaman withdraws in a rage, and slams the door of his chariot, apparently all set to make tracks and keep going all the way to Damascus.

But his servants, for whatever reason and by whatever means, persuade him that – having come all this way, and invested so much trouble in the trip – surely it's worth biting his lip, buttoning down his pride and calling in at the Jordan on the way past. After all, what does he have to lose? If that man had offered to put you through some complex ceremony, they say, then you'd have done it. Why miss out on the chance, since all he's actually asked you to do is something so simple. And the battle for Naaman's soul really takes place here between verses 13 and 14. Will he take the risk, make himself even more vulnerable to having been made to look foolish and follow the prophet's instructions, delivered to him second hand? Or will he retain what remains of his dignity, make himself feel better at least for a short while by treating the very idea with the contempt it seems to deserve, and burn up the tarmac to the border?

This is Naaman's moment of truth: his encounter with the peculiar grace of God, approaching him through the prophet's ostensibly rude behaviour, challenging to its roots Naaman's sense of self-importance and power, and confronting him with a choice. Just how badly do you want this Naaman? Are you willing to risk being made vulnerable, being made to seem foolish if this fails? Are you prepared to clutch at this one seemingly unpromising straw, to see whether, against all reasonable expectations, it will bear the weight of your need? Are you prepared to risk all the implications that will follow if it actually succeeds? After all, if *this* works, you won't have any choice about how you account for it. No ritual technology to point to. Not even the prophet's own hypnotic stare or healing hands. If *this* works – just you, and the river, open to public gaze – then you're going to have to reckon with the reality of something, someone, much bigger than yoga, aromatherapy and psychosomatic therapy.

Well – in a moment of madness, Naaman decides to give it a go. He drives to the Jordan and, in front of all his men, leaves his power and wealth and influence on the river bank with his clothes and his sword, and wades in. And, we read, 'he went down and immersed himself seven times in the Jordan, according to the word of the man of God; his flesh was restored like the flesh of a young boy, and he was clean.' And it goes on to tell how Naaman's response is one in which he is wholly transformed, not just outwardly but inwardly. After all, the leprosy was only part of his problem. It was symbolic, and perhaps symptomatic, of a deeper decay in his soul caused by power, success and pride. He returns to Elisha's house, this time in a quite different mood, and declares his desire to serve the God who has taken hold of him and shaken him into his right mind through this bizarre incident. And he returns to his own country, carrying with him two loads of earth, to serve as a 'piece' of Israel on which he can build his own small shrine, and worship the LORD.

It's a conversion story. And while it comes to us across cultures and across millennia, it also reminds us that there are some things that never change. When the God of the Bible wants to lay hold of someone and turn their lives around, he often has to do so in the strangest of ways, thwarting expectations, coming upon them incognito, unidentifiable, and taking them at their most vulnerable. Because it is only when we are caught by surprise, reduced to our bare essentials, and perhaps called to take a step that in the world's eyes can only seem to be foolish, that we can reckon with

what really counts in life, and what is, and is not, worth invest-
ing our allegiance in.

> Come, Lord, when grace has made me meet
>   Thy blessed face to see;
> For if Thy work on earth be sweet,
>   What will Thy glory be!
>
> Then I shall end my sad complaints,
>   And weary, sinful days;
> And join with the triumphant saints,
>   To sing JEHOVAH'S praise.[1]

... in remembering who we are

(Nehemiah 4, and 10 – 13)

The book of Nehemiah tells a story that is, as they say, 'based on events in real life' and in which resemblance to characters in real life is anything but accidental or unintended. That's not true of all good stories, even in the Bible; but it is true of this one. Nehemiah, Artaxerxes, Sanballat and the rest are all bona fide flesh-and-blood personalities from the pages of history, rather than the mere skilful products of an ancient literary imagination. It doesn't strictly matter, of course, for our purposes whether these things happened or not, or happened in this precise way or not (although clearly it may matter a great deal for some other purposes). It is the story itself, the characters we meet in it, the plot which unfolds in it, which are important; and questions about its merits and impact as a story can be asked and answered independently of questions about the extent of its historical accuracy. Nonetheless, the fact that it is at least substantially based on a 'true life' situation encourages us to set it in a wider context, to trespass beyond the horizons of the book of Nehemiah itself, and to locate the story it recounts within the wider story of Israel's history under God. For the book itself presupposes this, and takes it for granted that this history will be familiar to its readers. It begins with a Jewish civil servant in the Persian court; but it supposes that we will be well aware – in broad terms at least – how he comes to be there at all. So, in order to avail ourselves of what the story has to offer, it would be worthwhile reminding ourselves of these things.

Although it is tucked away in the middle of our Old Testament, the book of Nehemiah actually tells a story that belongs at the very end, just before the Old Testament itself, as it were, falls silent, and settles down to wait to see how God might bring his ancient promises to Israel to fulfilment. But the end of the Old Testament's story is anything but quietistic, a dampening down of the flames of expectation in readiness for a period of patient stocktaking in Israel's life. On the contrary, the story ends on a high note, a note of urgent and almost impatient expectation and readiness, looking for and finding God's hand at work in the midst of historical events, as a prelude to the coming great and glorious Day of the LORD. And Nehemiah's story is a pivotal one in all this.

The curtain comes down on the Old Testament's story in the latter half of the fifth century BC. Just a few scenes earlier in the action – about a hundred years or so – the exile with which the kingdom of Judah had been threatened by a string of well-known prophets (see, e.g., Jer. 25) finally became reality, as the Babylonians plundered Jerusalem, destroyed the city, including the king's palace and the Temple, and route-marched a signifi-cant proportion of the nation's populace hundreds of miles across the desert into captivity (see 2 Kings 25; Jer. 52), leaving behind only the poorest and least skilled to fend for themselves. Politics being a fickle business, though, the imperial winds soon blew in a new direction, and within 20 years Susa, capital of the Persian Empire (and in modern-day Iran) replaced Babylon as the centre of power in the Middle East. The Persian ruler Cyrus was rather better disposed toward his Jewish subjects than Nebuchadnezzar had been, and in 538 BC he allowed large numbers of them to make their way back across the desert to Jerusalem, and to begin work on rebuilding the ruined Temple (see Ezra 1 – 4.) This per-missive repatriation was seen – by people of Nehemiah's genera-tion a century later, for example – as the beginning of God's promise through prophets such as Isaiah and Jeremiah to restore his people to Zion. This promise was closely wedded in Israel's mind to others, such as the promise to raise up a great leader to rule over the nation as King David did of old, a ruler who would establish justice, who would be given the names Wonderful Counsellor, Prince of Peace, Mighty God, Everlasting Father. The return of God's people to Jerusalem, then, was no small matter, but seen as the herald of even greater things to come.

And so we come to Nehemiah himself as we meet him at our story's outset: not in Jerusalem, but in Susa, some 800 miles or so to the east, and more or less a century after the first Jews had begun to trickle home from exile. Although he is a Jew (and, as the story reveals, a faithful and devout one) Nehemiah is among those who, for one reason or another, have remained behind in Persia. His parents, grandparents and great-grandparents were probably all born and all died outside the Promised Land although, as the opening of Nehemiah's story here tells us, the distance did not dissuade some traffic to and fro, and devout Jews might well have made the long and difficult journey whenever they could in order to attend such religious festivals as Passover, which was once again being celebrated in Jerusalem. Despite the hopes and expectations sparked by the rebuilt Temple, though, it seems that little has happened to encourage those looking for signs of the nation's effective rebirth as a spiritual as well as a political entity. On the contrary, the news Hanani bears with him from Jerusalem to the imperial capital is sufficient to cast Nehemiah into a deep mood of depression. Far from signs of hope and promise, the Jews in Jerusalem are 'in great trouble and shame; the wall of Jerusalem is broken down, and its gates have been destroyed by fire'.

This sounds like bad news even at first blush. But in fact there is much more to it than at first meets the modern reader's eye. It may seem to be getting upset rather too easily to be cast down, as Nehemiah is, into weeping, mourning and fasting by a bad report on the state of the city's fabric. But, despite appearances, Nehemiah is not a melancholic. The walls of the city were for the Jews a powerful symbol as well as a material reality, a symbol bound up with the nation's well-being under God. They had been built by King Solomon in the golden age of Israel's history, and they stood effectively as a sign of the wholeness and integrity of the people of Israel, and of its being set apart from the nations; a visible marker of an invisible but nonetheless real difference or separateness. A reminder that while she was inescapably and significantly in the midst of the world, Israel was in an important and deep sense not 'of' the world, did not really *belong* to the world with its standards and ways of seeing and doing things. Conversely, therefore, the physical reality of Jerusalem's walls torn or broken down was for Jews redolent of an underlying spiritual and moral decay among the people, of the mixing of the LORD's standards with those of other gods. And it was at the same time an image of judgement. 'Now I will tell you what I am going to do to my vineyard' says God in Isaiah 5; 'I will break down its wall, and it will be trampled'. The literary image became more than just an image when, in 587BC, Nebuchadnezzar's army duly arrived and 'set fire to God's temple, and broke down the wall of Jerusalem'. Given all this, it is hardly surprising that the project of rebuilding the city walls came to lie at the heart of Israel's messianic hope. So in Ezekiel 48:30f. we find a complex and detailed account of the dimensions of the walls which will be built in the New Jerusalem, an image eventually picked up and developed by the author of the Christian book of Revelation (21:12f.). And in Isaiah 44, this same hopeful leitmotif of the restoration of Jerusalem from its ruins is associated directly with the edict of Cyrus and the return of the Jews from the Persian exile.

We can see, then, how the theme of the broken-down walls and their rebuilding would have evoked memories and expectations; expectations of the coming of God's chosen and anointed ruler who would come to save Israel and to establish God's kingdom among the nations. This was what the Jews of Nehemiah's day believed might now be happening. This is what Nehemiah himself is waiting eagerly to hear about as he carries on his day-to-day business so far from his homeland. No wonder Hanani's words hit him so hard. They offer news of decay and neglect of a deep-rooted nature, where Nehemiah is hoping instead to hear of the growth of God's kingdom. Clearly something has gone badly wrong, and something serious needs to be done. Now, if at any time, the great leader promised by God seems to be needed. But there is no sign of the clouds parting, or choirs of angels appearing, or of God planning to do anything very much soon. The indications that he might have been going to do so have all come to nothing, or so it seems.

But then, as Nehemiah turns in his desperation to prayer, to confession of his people's sins and the righteousness of God's

judgement upon them, and to a direct appeal to God's promise
not to abrogate his covenant with Israel but finally to restore and
renew it, so it gradually dawns on him that he, Nehemiah, might
just have some part to play in doing what needs to be done. It's
one of the odd things about prayer, especially intercession in
which we are asking God to do something, that it sometimes
takes a while for us to get around to asking whether we might be
part (however small a part) of the answer to our own petition.
And the bigger the problem or the situation we face, the longer it
seems to take us. We want thunderbolts, or smoke, or miraculous
interventions (and occasionally we may get them); but very often
God's way forward seems to need more mundane and down to
earth hands to get dirty; and, since we're the ones doing the asking, ours might find themselves at the front of the queue for consideration. To pray is to commit ourselves to doing whatever the
answer to our prayer may demand of us. And Nehemiah, facing
what was, after all, a rather considerable circumstance, suddenly
realizes that even he might have a role to play in all this, although
it is doubtful whether, at the end of chapter 1, he can have any
idea just what part that might be going to entail.

Like Esther in the story we shall consider in chapter 8,
Nehemiah is one of those otherwise insignificant individuals in
the Bible who find themselves transfigured into key characters in
the story by virtue of what, humanly speaking, is the sheer acci-
dent of being in a particular place at a particular time. (From
God's point of view, of course, it is the right place at the right time,
and Nehemiah's being there is far from accidental!) So, here, having had his passion for the plight of the Jews and the promise of
God stirred up to fever pitch, Nehemiah goes off to work at his job
as – as it happens in the providence of God – cupbearer to the
Emperor Artaxerxes! And he just *happens* to be asked by his master why he is looking so miserable. And he just *happens* to mention
the predicament of his people on the empire's most westerly
shores. And then Nehemiah prays one of those short, impulsive
'arrow' prayers with his eyes still open ('Please God, let him say,
"Okay then, off you go then and sort it all out" – as if!'). And
Artaxerxes says, 'Okay then, off you go and sort it all out'. So
Nehemiah learns something about the potential hazards of prayer,
as well as its potential benefits. Often they are the same thing.

This more or less brings us to the point of the story where we joined it in chapter 4. And here we find Nehemiah already back in Jerusalem, with the Emperor's blessing and authority and resources to get on with the rebuilding work, and having now announced his intention to do so to his fellow Jews. But what follows is hardly a tale of unambiguous welcome and assistance. There are those who are disturbed by what Nehemiah is doing, and who scheme and plot to undermine his efforts, even, eventually, to get rid of him through violent means. Clearly, then, steps towards the establishment of God's kingdom are not ones that are welcome in every quarter. And here they attract a powerful and dangerous opposition. So where exactly does the opposition come from?

Well, we can allow the character of Sanballat to stand as convenient representative of those others also mentioned in the story. Historians tell us that he was Governor of Samaria, and so he had good political reasons for feeling that his patch was being trespassed upon by Nehemiah with his personal mandate from the Emperor. But there is more to Sanballat's resistance than this. His name betrays a Babylonian lineage. But there had been a deliberate and wholesale occupation of the land by Babylonians many generations earlier during the exile, and Sanballat was probably born and bred either in Israel or Samaria. So he was a local, and not a foreigner, at least in geographical terms. He even seems to have grown up within some sort of Jewish religion. 'Some sort of', because it is likely to have been anything but what Nehemiah would have recognized as full-blooded Jewish belief and practice. As often happens when invasion and occupation mix up cultures, strange liaisons had emerged between bits of one culture and bits of others. And religion is no exception to such mixing, but – on the contrary – often a prime site for it, as practical adjustments and accommodations to cultural plurality are deliberately made, initially for reasons of tolerant generosity and harmonious coexistence, and later, perhaps, in order to provide apparently deep ethnic roots for a relatively recent and shallow political identity. So, while Sanballat had named his children after Israel's God, he clearly does not consider himself to be a Jew *in the same sense* as Nehemiah is. He views Nehemiah as some sort of throwback to an earlier, less attractive, age and way of seeing things. So Sanballat's position is, in the story, an uncomfortable one. This is his home, and the way of life to which he feels attached and within which he feels comfortable. And now Nehemiah is threatening to muscle in on his territory, and to disrupt it all by re-establishing a much more rigorous and far-reaching version of the older religion, which he (Sanballat) had hoped was all but dying out in place of a more tolerant and pluralistic alternative. The sort of confident and abrupt reproach embodied in Nehemiah's words in chapter 2 verse 20 ('The God of heaven is the one who will give us success, . . . but you have no share or claim or historic right in Jerusalem') must be hurtful to him, and is certainly designed to provoke him into action. And so his ire is aroused, and he seeks every opportunity to disadvantage Nehemiah's cause, determined to banish from the land the sort of old fashioned conservatism that Nehemiah represents.

Later in the story, when Nehemiah is already victorious, when the law of God has been read aloud in the city, and a ceremony of national and public recommitment to the covenant has been held, we find that the issue of purity – racial, cultural and religious – is faced head on, and responded to with some heavy-handed ideology which we may find far from easy either to understand or to stomach. In chapter 10 verse 28, we read of those who, having heard the law read aloud, 'have separated themselves from the peoples of the land to adhere to the law of God'. What exactly this entails is not specified, though the book of Ezra (which recounts some of the same story) suggests that some families are deliberately dissolved, with women and children being sent away because of their ethnic origins (see Ezra 10:2f.). What is clear is that a pressure to disentangle the liaisons established over several generations is deliberately brought to bear as a matter of official policy in every sphere of the people's lives. This encouragement of an 'us and them' mentality, of course, can throw up all manner of problems within communities, as family member is set now against family member, neighbour against neighbour, and colleague against colleague. Parallels with the recent history of Serbs and Croats in the former Yugoslavia or Hutus and Tutsis in Rwanda need to be handled with great care, and may evoke some inappropriate associations that do not fit the biblical case very precisely. Nonetheless the comparison may be illuminating at certain levels, and certainly indicates the worst prospects for such political dynamics. To read the end of Nehemiah 13, the very denouement of the story, is certainly to be confronted with a form of mild ethnic cleansing (mild in the sense that – unlike the Balkan and Rwandan instances – it stops short of deliberate violence and murder) in a bid to recover a clear sense of Israel's own identity in the world under God.

As readers whose sensibilities have been shaped by modern liberal democracies, we may find that the tenor of these chapters runs wholly counter to our social and political instincts, and even distances our sympathies somewhat from the story. Several things, though, need to be said before we rush to judgement. First, these chapters are not offered to us as a model for contemporary political practice, but recount an extreme crisis facing the nation of Israel at a particular and crucial moment in her history. Nor, of course, does this story capture the whole or even the most important parts of the picture of Israel's predisposition towards other races, religions and cultures. In ancient times, indeed, she had been required by God to care for 'the stranger within your borders', and this prescription had thoroughly theological roots: 'the LORD your God is God of gods and Lord of lords . . . who is not partial and takes no bribe, who executes justice for the orphan and the widow, and loves the strangers, providing them with food and clothing. You shall also love the stranger, for you were strangers in the land of Egypt' (Deut. 10:17-19). Except when they were suffering from a very short memory, the Jews knew all about what it meant to be part of an ethnic and religious minority, suffering oppression at the hands of those who enjoyed privilege and power. Furthermore, in the LORD'S own treatment of her, Israel had a divine example to follow in protecting and, where necessary, rescuing those who found themselves in such a predicament. Unlike Egypt, Israel was to be a generous, tolerant and accommodating nation, one whose character corresponded closely to that of her God. And yet the very next verse of this passage in Deuteronomy sounds a cautionary note: 'You shall fear the LORD your God, him alone you shall worship; to him you shall hold fast, and by his name you shall swear' (Deut. 10:20).

There are moments and situations where generosity can turn into compromise, tolerance amount to indifference, and accommodation lead to the effective exaltation of principles contradictory to a community's own distinctive identity, and therefore putting its continued existence (and possibly its value to others) under threat. And if it was true that the God of the Exodus was a God who set his people free to be a generous and life-giving community, it was also true that she could only be and do this while she remained faithful in her relationship with him and faithful to the shape of the covenanted way of existence prescribed in his commandments. And having 'called her out' from among the nations precisely in order to bless the nations by her distinctive existence, the LORD repeatedly calls Israel to maintain her distinctness at all costs. The link between intermarriage and the blurring of cultural and religious boundaries is one which the Old Testament depicts as a concern familiar to Israel as far back as memory would stretch. So in Genesis 28 we read how

> Isaac called Jacob and blessed him and charged him, 'You shall not marry one of the Canaanite women. Go at once to Paddan-aram, to the house of Bethuel, your mother's father; and take as wife from there one of the daughters of Laban, your mother's brother. May God Almighty bless you and make you fruitful and numerous, that you may become a company of peoples. May he give to you the blessing of Abraham, to you and to your offspring with you, so that you may take possession of the land where you now live as an alien – land that God gave to Abraham.' (Gen. 28:1-4)

Here we are confronted by another key moment in Israel's story. And here again we find an ironic and seemingly paradoxical juxtaposition of concerns. Isaac's concern is that his son Jacob (who will become 'Israel', father to the twelve tribes) should not put at risk the blessing which God gave to Abraham, and which will be transmitted to and through his progeny, so urges him to 'keep it in the family', and thereby avoid the danger of it being diluted or even haemorrhaging away as the result of conflicting domestic interests. Yet what is at stake here, ultimately, is not the blessing of Jacob and his offspring, but the blessing *in and through* them of all nations. Cultural, religious and racial distinctives – secured here through what may indeed look to our eyes a somewhat blinkered and elitist attitude to others – are not finally to exclude others at all, but precisely to incorporate them in the blessing of God's salvation, which is 'for all'. But Israel did not need any sociology textbook to tell them what would most likely happen to their distinctive faith and practices if they permitted the sign of circumcision to be cheapened by mixing it with uncircumcision in widespread intermarriage. From the moment a Canaanite girl fluttered her eyes at a Jewish boy (or a Jewish girl at a Canaanite boy!), the fear was always that a crack might appear in the dyke, which would, in time, become a trickle, and then a stream, and then a flood in which God's call to Israel would be washed away and forgotten.

This same set of concerns is expressed very concretely in the renewal of God's covenant with Israel in Exodus 34, where – in the immediate wake of the incident with the Golden Calf – the LORD says to Moses:

> Take care not to make a covenant with the inhabitants of the land to which you are going, or it will become a snare among you. You shall tear down their altars, break their pillars, and cut down their sacred poles (for you shall worship no other god, because the LORD . . . is a jealous God). You shall not make a covenant with the inhabitants of the land, for when they prostitute themselves to their gods and sacrifice to their gods, someone among them will invite you, and you will eat of the sacrifice. And you will take wives from among their daughters for your sons, and their daughters who prostitute themselves to their gods will make your sons also prostitute themselves to their gods.' (Exod. 34:12-16)

The same prescription is stated negatively in Deuteronomy 7: 'Do not intermarry with (the nations) . . . for that would turn away your children from following me. . . . For you are a people holy to the LORD your God' (Deut. 7:3, 6).

All this provides an important backdrop to the admittedly stringent and unpleasant social measures decreed and overseen by Nehemiah. Cultural accommodation and idolatry were precisely the things that had led to God's judgement upon Judah in invasion and exile just a hundred years or so ago. And now it seems as though the generations who have remained in Jerusalem since have learned nothing, but have if anything committed the trespasses of the past over again with interest added, allowing their identity as the people of God to become thoroughly blurred through an inappropriate intercourse with those whose hearts, like their bodies, remain uncircumcised. What Nehemiah, Ezra and others are forced to reckon with in this situation is the fact that the task of repairing the ruins which faces them is going to have more than a purely architectural dimension. The forced disentanglement of races is in effect a replication on another level of the physical rebuilding of the walls earlier in the story. It's not pleasant, and it's not a prescription for anything but the most urgent of circumstances. But the most urgent of circumstances is precisely what this story is about. What is at stake is nothing less than the survival of the nation's identity as a people called out by God, and hence of those promises and purposes in history which that identity embodies. The painful disruption that Nehemiah's policy causes to the people is a measure of the extent to which this identity has been allowed to be obscured, and the costliness of God's gracious redeeming of it so that the promise may be carried forward rather than lost.

Nehemiah's God is also our God, the God known to us in Jesus. And whatever else it may be, this is a story about the implications and possible costs of discovering, perhaps recovering, our distinctive identity as those whom this same God has called into fellowship with himself, but who live in a world which either resists that call or else prefers to try and negotiate its own terms with God. So, while the story certainly doesn't offer us a political or social blueprint for life in a plural society in the third millennium, it does draw our attention importantly to issues of faith and identity – and to the messy consequences of compromise – which apply just as surely in our day as in Nehemiah's, and never more so than in identifiably plural contexts. And as Christian readers of the text, we should neither overlook nor underestimate the fact that the New Testament also cautions against certain sorts or levels of accommodation with unbelievers. In particular, Paul echoes the Old Testament's proscription of 'intermarriage'. 'Do not be mismatched with unbelievers' he writes, 'For . . . what does a believer share with an unbeliever?'

(2 Cor. 6:14-15). Obviously they may hold *some things* in common; perhaps many things, and perhaps some significant things. But the insight toward which Paul's question directs us is that the levels of commitment properly involved both in Christian faith and in marriage are so fundamental and the commitments so all-embracing that where the two cannot effectively become inter-woven – so that commitment of marriage is itself in effect a dimension of one's commitment to Christ – then sooner or later they are likely to compete unhelpfully for the same territories of the heart, and one or other will suffer damage as a result. With the likelihood of such circumstances arising, Paul is saying, avoidance is a much better strategy than retrieval.

Here, though, it is equally interesting to note what he has to say about those whose commitment to Christ first arises within an existing marriage, and where the partner in the marriage remains an unbeliever. For the sake of the marriage, and for the sake of any children in the marriage, he indicates, so long as the unbelieving partner consents to the continuation, the marriage should contin-ue and will be 'sanctified' by the presence of Christ in it (see 1 Cor. 7:12-16). Given the question 'what do these share in common?', we might have expected an exhortation parallel to that of Nehemiah to Israel to 'separate yourselves out from your entan-glements with the nations'. But Paul is dealing with the regulari-ties of Christian living, rather than a crisis point in Israel's history, and here the welfare and concerns of families can be afforded a more significant priority, and a more flexible attitude be adopted towards liaisons which, while perhaps not ideal, may yet be blessed and redeemed by their association with Christ. No doubt Christians involved in such marriages will face more directly the challenges and the risks of compromise and an erosion of their commitment to Christ; but all Christians will in any case face such challenges and risks in one situation or another (and not least in marriage even when both parties are believers – see 1Cor. 7:32f.); and, as Paul himself surmises, the patient presence of faithful dis-cipleship within such a family may be the very instrument God uses to draw other members of that family to himself.

In fact, the tension reflected throughout Paul's letters, and throughout the New Testament as a whole, is between recognition that, on the one hand Christians are called to be different from the crowd, to be 'separate', holy to the LORD, of the Spirit rather than the flesh, and on the other hand they must be immersed thoroughly in the world as what will often be an odd, counter-cultural and potentially transforming presence – light in the midst of darkness, salt to purify and preserve a world in danger of going bad, and so on. The difference which Christian identity makes should never finally be at the world's expense, but for the world's sake and its good. In the world's midst, Christians nonetheless do not finally 'belong' to it, and this alien status must sometimes be expressed in distinctive patterns of life, patterns which amount to disentanglement from the world's expectations and values. Disentangling, though, needs to be and can only be done to things which are very close to one another to begin with; light needs to be placed in the middle of the darkness in order to be noticed; and salt that sits in a pile away from that which needs to be preserved is of no practical use whatever. So the sort of 'separateness' to which Christians are called certainly cannot amount to 'having nothing whatever to do with' unbelievers or the unbelieving culture of our age. But there are different ways of 'having to do with'. And what the story of Nehemiah reminds us is that there will be occasions and situations when, despite our being immersed to the very hilt in the world, the most important thing will be for the borders, the boundaries of our identity to be re-established and marked out, for the walls to be rebuilt, so that it is clear just who is on the inside and who is on the outside, even when (as will usually be the case) it is painful to us and to others to have to do this.

Our Father in heaven,
may your name be hallowed.
may your kingdom come, and your will be done
on earth as in heaven.
We ask you to show us where the broken walls and burned gates
are
in our lives as individuals and as the church,
and we pray that you would pour out your Holy Spirit
enabling us to restore them,
that all might be drawn to the light of your redeeming love.
Amen.

8

. . . in the demands of the circumstances

(Esther 4:1 – 5:8)

Although our focus is going to be at the critical point in the story of Esther at which Esther herself takes decisive action – in chapters 4 and 5 – we must first recall the story so far. It is set in the fifth century BC in Susa, one of the two capitals of the mighty Persian Empire. As a matter of fact Susa, in modern Iran, is the furthest point east that is the location for any biblical narrative, just as Rome is the furthest point west in which any biblical story is set. The Persian Empire stretched from north-west India to Ethiopia. It was the largest empire there had ever been, encompassing most of the known world. Therefore the most powerful man in the world, ruling this vast empire, was Ahasuerus, king of kings, who had his winter palace in Susa. In theory Ahasuerus was an absolute despot: his word alone ruled the world. In practice, as we soon discover in reading Esther, Ahasuerus was a weak man, unable to make decisions for himself, dependent on his advisers and easily manipulated by them.

By this time Jews were living in many parts of the Persian Empire, including Susa itself. The two heroes of the story are members of the Jewish community in Susa: Esther and her cousin Mordecai. Since Esther's parents had died when she was young, Mordecai had brought her up. The other essential thing to know about Esther is that she was stunningly beautiful.

The first part of Esther's story has a kind of fairy-tale quality: ordinary Jewish girl becomes the wife of the emperor. Ahasuerus was in need of a wife, having got annoyed with his previous wife and banished her from the court. Not that he was really short of wives. At least, like any oriental monarch, he had a harem full of concubines. The more powerful the king, the greater the number of his concubines. But Ahasuerus wanted, not just another concubine, but a queen. A queen had to be special. She need not be especially intelligent or especially good at anything, but she had to be especially beautiful. So the king's advisers tell him what he must do. (He would probably never have thought of it himself.) Royal officials throughout the empire are to search out the most beautiful girls and bring them all to Susa for a kind of ancient Miss World contest. Some contest it turns out to be! The keeper of the harem himself chooses the best of them, and they spend twelve months getting ready before the king himself even sets eyes on them. Twelve months of cosmetic treatment in the palace beauty parlours.

Among these girls is Esther, who quickly becomes the harem-keeper's favourite. She must be very young. Such a beautiful girl would not have remained unmarried for very long after puberty. She must be only 12 or 13 when she joins the royal harem. Of course, she has no real choice about it. In Susa you do what the king's officers say (at least usually: we shall notice a striking exception shortly). But Esther keeps quiet about being Jewish. Her cousin Mordecai has advised her to do so, no doubt because the Jews were a despised and marginal group in Persian society. Evidently Mordecai does not want Esther's Jewishness to stand in the way of her chances of becoming queen. Why should he want her to become queen? The palace of the pagan emperor is hardly the place for a good Jewish girl, one might have thought. Maybe Mordecai is just ambitious for her. More likely, he has the idea it might be useful for the Jewish people to have a representative so close to the king, someone who might be able to protect their interests.

At last, after a year, it is Esther's turn to go to the king. The king, we learn 'loved Esther more than all the other women; of all the virgins she won his favour and devotion, so that he set the royal crown on her head and made her queen' (2:17). He gives a huge banquet for her – one of several in the book. The story seems to move from one banquet to another. We should be imagining the sumptuous luxury and extravagance of this imperial court. Thus far the fairy tale: not quite rags to riches, but ordinary Jewish girl to queen of the largest empire on earth. However, it's worth noticing that so far Esther has not really done anything. At every stage she has been told what to do. She does what her cousin tells her, as no doubt she had been doing all her life. Once in the harem she does what the harem-keeper tells her. When her time to go to the king comes, she could choose, we are told, anything she wanted to wear or to adorn herself, but in fact she takes only what the harem keeper advises her. This passive and obedient role is hardly surprising in a girl so young in the culture of that time. Moreover, there is no indication that her role as queen requires anything more than being beautiful and charming and available to the king whenever he wants her. Even as queen she does only what she is told. So far she has done nothing to justify having a book of the Bible named after her.

When Haman, the villain, enters the story, it suddenly becomes less like a charming fairy tale, more like the Third Reich. Haman is the original anti-Semite who first thought up a final solution to the problem of the Jews. Coming from a Miss World contest we find ourselves suddenly in sight of the gas chambers. Of course, we are still within the world of the oriental court. Haman is grand vizier of the empire, the man to whom the king is happy to delegate his power, glad to have someone to trust and rely on, relieved not to have to make decisions himself. Unfortunately Ahasuerus cannot make a good decision even in choosing his grand vizier. Haman is a man of vast ambition and complete self-obsession, grotesquely jealous of his own status and dignity. He persuades the king to command that Haman should always be greeted by all the king's servants with the most elaborate obeisance, bowing down with head to the ground at his feet, the ancient gesture of submission. One man refuses to do so: Mordecai the Jew. We are not told why, but we guess that Mordecai is one of those Jews who believes it wrong to give to a pagan ruler the kind of absolute submission that is owed by God's own people only to God. We guess that, but the story says nothing about God – a fact to which we shall return.

Haman is furious. He is furious every time he walks past this Jew who obstinately will not bow down to him. We observe the mounting fury of a megalomaniac who, we are told, 'thought it beneath his dignity to lay hands on Mordecai alone.' So, having learned who Mordecai's people were, Haman plots 'to destroy all the Jews throughout the whole kingdom of Ahasuerus' (3:6). That means practically all the Jews there were in the world. In revenge for one man's insubordination, one slight to his honour, Haman plots genocide. And he can do it. This is virtually the only time in history when all Jews lived within a single political entity in which one man's despotic will prevailed. That will is Ahasuerus's, of course, but it will not be difficult for Haman his favourite to persuade him. Here are the chilling words of the first recorded expression of a subsequently standard anti-Semitic accusation:

> Then Haman said to King Ahasuerus, 'There is a certain people scattered and separated among the peoples in all the provinces of your kingdom; their laws are different from those of every other people, and they do not keep the king's laws, so that it is not appropriate for the king to tolerate them. If it pleases the king, let a decree be issued for their destruction, and I will pay ten thousand talents of silver . . . into the king's treasuries.' (3:8-9)

The king does not even bother to find out who this people are. All he wants to know about the problem is that Haman is taking care of it. So the well-oiled machinery of the empire's government immediately starts moving. An edict from the king, written to Haman's specification, is carried by the empire's famously efficient governmental courier system to every province. On a specific date the king's subjects are to massacre the Jews in their neighbourhood, every Jew to the last woman and child, and – the necessary incentive – they can plunder the Jews' possessions. Before the Second World War, commentators on Esther sometimes regarded this as a ridiculously improbable scenario, the product of some kind of Jewish persecution complex. After the Holocaust, Esther reads rather differently. It is worth remembering that in the Nazi death camps, where the Jews had no scriptures, they wrote out the book of Esther from memory in order to recite it on the feast of Purim, the annual Jewish festival when Esther is read.

We reach the part of the story that is our focus, and here we must especially notice the change that happens to Esther herself. Up to 4:11 she is still the obedient girl who has to be told what to do by Mordecai. He urges her to go to speak to the king. When Esther says, 'I can't, it's not allowed,' she is caught between obeying her guardian and obeying her husband the king. She is being obliged to decide something. Can she risk the king's wrath? Then, with Mordecai's last message to her, comes the turning-point in the story as a whole and the turning-point in Esther's own story:

> Mordecai told them to reply to Esther, 'Do not think that in the king's palace you will escape any more than all the other Jews. For if you keep silence at such a time as this, relief and deliverance will rise for the Jews from another quarter, but you and your father's family will perish. Perhaps you have come to royal dignity for just such a time as this.' (4:13-14).

Esther's rise to the unique position she is in is not something she has done but something that has happened to her. Perhaps, Mordecai suggests, she has been put there for just such a time as this, when her people are threatened with genocide and she may be the one person in a position to avert disaster. That insight changes Esther. Suddenly she sees she must take action herself. She takes on Mordecai's advice not just in the sense of obeying him the way she always has done, but in the sense of taking on the role he has shown her now falls to her. What she makes of that role is now up to her. She must decide how to go about it. She must summon her courage and her intelligence. She must take bold and risky initiatives. All at once Esther grows up. She is her own person at last.

What she does immediately is tell Mordecai what to do. Surely this is the first time in her life she has told her guardian what to do. It will also be the first time that 'Mordecai went away and did everything as Esther had ordered him' (4:17). In order to realize where this new development is leading, we can anticipate and observe that by the end of the story Esther is issuing edicts for the whole Jewish people. The institution of the feast of Purim, commemorating the events of this story, takes place by the command of 'Queen Esther', – as she is then called (9:29-32). From the end of chapter 4 onwards Esther becomes really the queen, not just the king's wife bound to obey him and supply his pleasure, but a person in authority herself, taking initiative and responsibility.

It is at the beginning of chapter 5 that she is first called 'Queen Esther' (5:2). This is the point at which she takes her life in her hands and begins the task of changing the king's mind. It is the very difficult task of countering Haman's influence over the king, which is, as we know, very considerable. All Ahasuerus really wants is an easy life. So Esther takes her time. Even when the king, besotted with her as he is, offers to grant her request, whatever it is, even to half his kingdom, she takes her time. It is the sort of thing oriental kings say when they want to sound extravagantly generous, but does Ahasuerus really mean it? Esther is anxious not to bungle her task. She wants to wait for the right moment. So she invites the king and Haman to a banquet. The king repeats his offer. She puts it off again. Another banquet – tomorrow . . . Readers who do not already know the story may read on in the book of Esther itself. At this point we stop following the story and go back to those words of Mordecai that constitute the turning-point of the plot, the message that precipitates the independent and courageous part that Esther is then able to assume.

We should notice, first, that Mordecai is entirely confident that, whether or not Esther does anything, the Jewish people will be saved from disaster somehow. Why is he so confident? Though he doesn't mention God, surely it is because he trusts God to keep his promises to his people and not let them perish. It is God's faithfulness to his promise and his people that means that, even without Esther's action, the Jews are ultimately safe. But, Mordecai says, who knows whether perhaps Esther has come to royal dignity for such a time as this? To make sense of those words, surely we have again to bring God into the picture. Mordecai is saying that, perhaps, God has put Esther where she is, with her influence over the king, because God has a purpose for her. It is this sense of a God-given vocation, surely, that Esther then takes on herself. It is the thought that this is what God has given her to do that now motivates her, enabling her to see there is something she really can do and inspiring her new-found courage and resourcefulness. Esther becomes her own person because she now sees herself as God's person.

Why then do neither Mordecai nor Esther actually mention God? It is difficult to read 4:14 without thinking of God, yet God is scrupulously unmentioned. This odd absence of God from the words of the text continues in what Esther says to Mordecai in verse 16. She talks about fasting: all the Jews in Susa are to fast, she and her maids will also fast. For any Jewish reader fasting implies prayer. The point of fasting was to assist prayer. It was a way of expressing to God how very seriously one meant one's prayer. Fasting had no value apart from prayer. So again God is *implied* in verse 16, but unmentioned.

In fact God never has been mentioned in the book of Esther and God never will be mentioned right up to the end of the book. This is an extraordinary feature of the book of Esther: a book of the Bible that never mentions God. (It is one of two such books: the other is the Song of Songs.) In the verses we have been considering the non-reference to God becomes conspicuous. One cannot help noticing it, at least if one has been reading the rest of the Bible.

Among the so-called deuterocanonical or apocryphal books there is another, longer version of the book of Esther. The main difference is that this apocryphal Esther puts in all the references to God that one might have expected. For example, at the beginning of chapter 5, before Esther embarks on her courageous attempt to save the Jews from genocide, the apocryphal Esther inserts a long prayer that Esther prays to God beseeching his aid in what she is going to do. This longer version of Esther is certainly a later version. It exists because people evidently felt, as we do, that there ought to be reference to God in Esther, and so someone expanded the book to make it much more overtly religious. But this just highlights for us again how unreligious, how apparently secular the original book of Esther is. Its studious lack of reference to the divine even extends from the God of Israel to encompass the pagan gods also. Nothing religious at all seems to happen at the Persian court. Anyone who knows anything about court banquets in the ancient world would expect there to be libations of wine poured to the gods and sacrifices offered, but nothing of the kind is mentioned in the accounts of the banquets in

Esther. Haman, the great enemy of the Jews, is not portrayed as an idolater who worships false gods. If Haman worships anyone, apparently it is himself.

So where is God in this secular world of the book of Esther? Significantly, this is a question we can also ask of our world, the world most of us live in most of the time, because there too God is rarely mentioned. Where is God in our apparently godless world?

Even though God is never mentioned in the book of Esther, Esther herself finds God in the midst of this apparently secular life, while, by the end of the book, God's people Israel have been delivered by God from the genocide that Haman plotted against them. In other words, although God is never mentioned, for readers of faith, readers who have learned from the rest of Scripture how to discern God in the midst of life, God is to be found between the lines of this narrative, perhaps not to start with, but certainly from the turning-point verse 4:14 onwards. For Esther herself, as we have seen, Mordecai's words in that verse are the decisive point. At that point she finds God in the demands and the challenge of the circumstances. In her unique place in life and in the circumstances of the moment, she recognizes there is something she has been given to do. But as the story develops we find that the deliverance of the Jews occurs not only because of Esther's courageous and resourceful action, but also through the particular collocation and coincidence of events that transpire – or that conspire, we might say, to ensure the salvation of God's people. For example, had it not happened that, on the night after the banquet Esther held for the king in chapter 5, Ahasuerus found himself unable to sleep and decided to pass the night by having the annals of his reign read to him, things would have worked out very differently. (Insomniacs among us may find this the only point in the narrative where we feel any sympathy for the king.) What turns out in the story of the book of Esther happens because Esther's own endeavours correlate with events over which she has no control and these two kinds of events combine to bring about the outcome. In other words, God is to be recognized, not only in the challenge of the circumstances to Esther herself to do something, but also in providence, in God's hand at work in the course of events. Esther's own resourcefulness is met by the resourceful hand of providence, prospering her actions and ensuring the successful outcome.

It is worth comparing the story of Esther with a much earlier and much better known story in which God's people were delivered from an attempt to destroy them – the Exodus. In the story of Israel's Exodus from Egypt God's presence and action are explicit, in fact highly evident. God speaks to Moses, sends the plagues of Egypt, parts the waters of the Red Sea. When we compare this with Esther, once again we notice the absence of God from explicit reference in Esther. In a sense we could say that Esther is a second Moses, but she has no experience like Moses' call by God, when God appeared to him in the burning bush; she has no miraculous authentication of her mission to show the king, like Aaron's staff that turned into a snake; there is no pillar of cloud leading the Jews to safety; there are no miraculous events in the salvation of the Jews in the book of Esther. Esther's call to act for God and his people is merely her recognition of the challenge of the circumstances to her; the miracles in Esther are the unexpected coincidences and collocations of events. Nothing in Esther makes God obviously perceptible as he was to Moses and the Israelites at the Exodus; rather it takes the eye of faith to notice God in the circumstances and events of life.

In this sense Esther's world is more like the world as most of us experience it most of the time than Moses' world is. It is not that burning-bush experiences and Exodus-type events never happen. But if we could not find God in our lives without such out-of-the-ordinary events, most of us would be at a loss much of the time. While it is hard to be entirely sure why the writer of the book of Esther decided to omit all explicit reference to God, it may be that he or she wished to suggest to readers how to perceive God in the seemingly godless world of everyday events, where there are no miraculous signposts pointing out to everyone where God is to be found. Reading the story we have to find God in it in the same way Esther did. We are not, as readers, given privileged information about what God is doing in the events, information Esther herself does not have. We readers are in the same position as Esther, learning, as it were, by sharing her experience. What we learn to do in Esther's story we must go on to do in our own lives.

One message chapters 4 and 5 of Esther have for us, then, is that we can and should find God in the circumstances in which we find ourselves, in the challenges they present to us, in the opportunities they offer for us to serve God and others. The challenge to hear a call of God in our circumstances does not always come as an unavoidable conviction or conclusion. Sometimes it comes as Mordecai's 'perhaps' and 'who knows?' – *'Who knows? Perhaps* you have come to royal dignity for such a time as this' (4:14). The hypothetical suggestion is enough to galvanize Esther into action.

Sometimes when people talk about obeying God and serving God, it can sound a bit too much like being a sort of automaton, as though God's will replaces our own human autonomy and initiative. In Esther's case we have noticed how the opposite happens. The challenge of the circumstances in which God speaks to her is what makes her for the first time her own person, draws out her unexpected capacities to take initiatives, to make plans, to act resourcefully and intelligently and with remarkable courage for a girl of fourteen who has hitherto always only done what people have told her to do. Being God's person is not the opposite of being one's own person. On the contrary, it is only as God's person, responsible and obedient to God, that one can truly be one's own person, realizing the freedom of action and the gifts and potentialities God has given us.

Finally, it is when, in our own smaller ways, we follow Esther's example in doing what we can for God that we shall also see God's hand in events that cannot be our doing. Providence is a very difficult doctrine to think about intellectually, but it is surely a quite essential doctrine for living in faith. God does not just leave us to do what we can, God prospers what we do, gives to our actions results they could not have just by themselves.

There is a balance to be struck here. On the one hand, like Esther we need to take confidence and courage to do what we believe God has called us and given us to do. On the other hand, we should also remember that it is God who gives whatever good may come of our actions. This is obvious enough really. In anything useful or good we may try to achieve, our intentions can always be frustrated by the course of events we cannot control. It is actually very dangerous to ignore that fact and to suppose, as politicians are sometimes tempted to do, that the success of what we attempt is wholly in our own control. That way lie dangerously inflated notions of our own power. In fact all we ever do is make a contribution which providence may prosper. Often providence far outruns what we might have expected possible or likely. God calls us to be responsible, resourceful, courageous, to put all we can into doing what we can, but he does not call us to be God. So we must find God in the challenge of the circumstances to do something, but we must also find God, with praise and thankfulness to him, in what continually turns out to be more than we could ever have achieved.

Lord of the world, keep our lives open to the truth of our
     circumstances,
keep us alert to the opportunities of our times,
give us discernment of your purposes in your world,
enable us to seize the moment for which you have brought
     us where we are,
give us something of Esther's courage and resourcefulness,
and surprise us with your providence in our seemingly
     godless world.

. . . in the futility of success

(Ecclesiastes 2)

A few years ago there was a serious train crash just outside Paddington station, one of London's rail termini. The passengers were commuters making their morning journey to London to work. Many were killed or badly injured; others escaped unharmed. Imagine two such passengers. One is a young woman, a student nurse, a lovely person, one of those radiant people who make everyone who knows them feel better. She is training as a nurse because she wants to devote her life to helping others. The other passenger, in the next carriage, is a man in late middle age, at the peak of a career in which he has been spectacularly successful in acquiring power and wealth through ruthless dedication to self-interest, unscrupulous business practices, doing much harm to others in the process. The train crash occurs. The woman dies in the inferno, all the great promise of her young life and all her good intentions of living it for good reduced to ashes. The man, in the next carriage, escapes unscathed, rather shaken, rather delayed – but he makes his usual way to the City, arriving in time for his scheduled business lunch with a client. His lucky escape becomes a good story he tells, relaxing over the after-dinner drinks.

This is the sort of story the author of the book of Ecclesiastes would tell if he were with us now. He would add it to his lifetime of disillusioned observation of the injustice and meaninglessness of life. Death and the arbitrariness of death defeat any attempt to make sense of life. This too, he would have said, is 'vanity' –

meaning: absurdity, futility, meaninglessness. Such pointless tragedy and such gross unfairness contribute to the conclusion with which he both begins and ends his book: 'Vanity of vanities, says the Teacher, all is vanity' (1:2; 12:8).

The story we are to consider now is the one he tells in the first person. We could call it: The story of the man who had everything but found it was nothing. The Teacher (as we will call him, following the NRSV's translation of his title) adopts the persona of King Solomon. This is a literary device. He is saying: Now imagine a man like Solomon, someone with all the power and all the wealth of Solomon, and all the wisdom of Solomon besides. Solomon was the man who had everything. Ruling the largest territory any king of Israel ever ruled, and with tributes and treasure pouring into his coffers from all over his empire and beyond, Solomon, surely, could have anything he wanted. Palaces, parks and pools, slaves and entertainers, concubines, banquets . . . every desire of all the senses he luxuriously indulged: 'Whatever my eyes desired I did not keep from them; I kept my heart from no pleasure' (2:10). Solomon had everything power and money could give, but was he satisfied? Did it bring him fulfilment in life? Not at all: 'Then I considered all that my hands had done and the toil I had spent in doing it, and again, all was vanity and a chasing after wind, and there was nothing to be gained under the sun' (2:11).

The pursuit of pleasure turned out to be chasing the wind. If you run after the wind trying to catch it, you may sometimes imagine you have it in your grasp, but you soon discover there is nothing there at all. While you are chasing it, there may seem to be purpose and meaning in life, the promise of happiness to be secured, but once you catch it there is only a void. While Solomon was planning his palaces, planting his orchards, seeking out the best singers and the most beautiful concubines, he was probably happier than when he had them all. What was he really wanting, what was missing in this life of luxury? He does not seem to be able to tell us. All he can say is that he has tried the pursuit of pleasure, he more than anyone has tried it out, and in the end he finds it hollow. The dazzling surface has nothing inside. It is all vanity, emptiness, absurdity, futility. But there is one revealing aspect of the story so far: notice the recurrent 'for myself' or 'myself' throughout his account of what he did: 'I built houses and planted vineyards for myself. I made myself gardens and parks. . . . I made myself pools. . . . I also gathered for myself silver and gold . . .' (2:4-8). The whole enterprise is entirely self-interested.

Is this story familiar? We might say that, whereas in ancient Israel Solomon was unusual in having the resources to try out the pursuit of material goods and the pleasures they give to its disillusioning end, in our extraordinarily affluent consumer society many people can do that. Ours is a society in which people are constantly encouraged to think that life is about getting more and more of what money can buy – a whole society of Solomons, a society chasing the wind. The difference from Solomon is that there are vastly more things and experiences to be bought than Solomon ever dreamed of. This makes it harder for modern hedonists to reach the conclusion that such things are inherently unable to give us what we most want in life. Dissatisfaction with them can always be taken to mean just that they have not satisfied us yet. Sensing the emptiness we merely think of more things to fill it: a new car, a conservatory, a holiday in the Himalayas, plastic surgery – the possibilities are endless.

The insatiability of desire, addiction to consumption – these are key characteristics of our society. The Teacher already knew about them: 'The eye is not satisfied with seeing, or the ear filled with hearing,' he says (1:8). 'Their eyes are never satisfied with riches' (4:8). 'The lover of money will not be satisfied with money, nor the lover of wealth, with gain. This also is vanity' (5:10). The urge to get and to have is inherently unsatisfiable, and the tragedy of our society is that it knows this and actually makes it the principle of economic life. A great deal of advertising aims to associate its product with images of ultimately satisfied desire: Buy this and you will be happy; buy this and you'll have the beautiful girl, the wonderful house, the admiration of your friends and colleagues, and so on. But at the same time advertising must feed on dissatisfaction, constantly stimulating desire, promising that elusive something you still have not found. There has to be a point at which we see through it all, a point at which we believe the sense of futility in our hearts rather than the lure of the ads and the products. The Teacher's story of the man who had everything is one way the Bible helps us to this realization. It saves us the fruitless exploration of it all for ourselves. It exposes what we all really know in our heart of hearts and what we can all observe in society around us when we are clear-sighted enough to do so.

A lot of us are chasing the wind. If we can see that in the addiction to consumption, we can also see it in the lure of success and the treadmill of achievement. Our society is no place for losers or slackers. To get on one must be single-minded in the pursuit of success, work long hours, take work home, cope with increasing stress – all for the money one has no time to spend or the family one has no time to be with. It is a crazy economy that divides us into the overworked winners and the unemployed losers. Also, of course, there is a key competitive element in it: the treadmill of achievement is often the compulsion to keep up or to get ahead. The Teacher knew about that too: 'Then I saw that all toil and all skill in work come from one person's envy of another. This also is vanity and a chasing after wind' (4:4). He also knew about workaholism and its futility: 'What do mortals get from all the toil and strain with which they toil under the sun? For all their days are full of pain, and their work is a vexation; even at night their minds do not rest. This also is vanity' (2:22-23).

A lot of us are chasing the wind. But we have not yet finished the Teacher's story. Solomon had everything: not only power and wealth and all they could bring him, but also wisdom. Discovering that the pursuit of pleasure was only chasing the wind, he turned to the way of wisdom. For this is how the traditions of the sages, the traditions of which the Teacher was a master, recommended people should live: Take to heart all those maxims in the book of Proverbs, all that good advice for fearing God and keeping out of trouble. Surely it is better to be wise than to be foolish? Solomon could hardly say otherwise and he joins in the traditional mockery of the fool. And yet . . . in the end does it make any difference whether one is wise or foolish? 'I perceived that the same fate befalls all of them. Then I said to myself, "What happens to the fool will happen to me also; why then have I been so very wise?" And I said to myself that this also is vanity' (2:14-15). Wisdom mocks folly, but wisdom is itself mocked by death. Whatever Solomon's achievements, there is no guaranteeing that they will survive him.

Everything comes to nothing in the end, as the Teacher's book itself does, ending in chapter 12 with a magnificent poetic evocation of death as the inevitable fate that renders everything futile and meaningless. 'Vanity of vanity, says the Teacher, all is vanity' (12:8): this is the conclusion of the matter (12:13).

The pursuit of success always runs into death in the end. To the successful person, their highest ambitions now tangibly within reach, there is always death to put the sceptical question: And then what? When you achieve what you have set out to achieve, then what? The Irish poet William Butler Yeats put it in this poem ('What Then?') of which the Teacher would certainly have approved:

> His chosen comrades thought at school
> He must grow a famous man;
> He thought the same and lived by rule,
> All his twenties crammed with toil;
> *'What then?' sang Plato's ghost. 'What then?'*
>
> Everything he wrote was read,
> After certain years he won
> Sufficient money for his need,
> Friends that have been friends indeed;
> *'What then?' sang Plato's ghost. 'What then?'*
>
> All his happier dreams came true –
> A small old house, wife, daughter, son,
> Grounds where plum and cabbage grew,
> Poets and Wits about him drew;
> *'What then?' sang Plato's ghost. 'What then?'*
>
> 'The work is done,' grown old he thought,
> 'According to my boyish plan;
> Let the fools rage, I swerved in naught,
> Something to perfection brought';
> *But louder sang that ghost, 'What then?'*[1]

The Teacher would have approved, but he had no answer to Plato's ghost. Only the inevitability of death that renders all achievements ultimately pointless, the more insistently the nearer one comes to it.

So does the man who had everything not come to any positive conclusions? Has he a recipe for a way of living that will not be chasing the wind? Only this: 'There is nothing better for mortals than to eat and drink, and find enjoyment in their toil' (2:24). This minimalist advice the Teacher repeats again and again through his book (3:12-13, 22; 5:18-20; 8:15; 9:9): Make the most of what little joy there is to be had in the short and wearisome life God gives us. Expect nothing more. Anything more is just chasing the wind. Do not expect to find meaning in life. The world is bewildering and impenetrable. Just enjoy it while you can, and especially be sure to enjoy it while you are young because as death approaches you will be less and less able to enjoy it. (This last point is the message of the famous concluding poem of the book: 12:1-8.)

It is not that the Teacher exempts anything from his overall verdict that all is vanity. The transient joys of everyday life are not some island of meaning in the great sea of life's absurdity. They are as meaningless as anything else. His point is that one just has to accept the absurdity and make the best of it. In its dis-illusioned minimalism the Teacher's advice is astonishingly post-modern. But can it really be lived?

There is one point in the Teacher's positive advice that is surely very important. The pleasures of life are a positive good in themselves. Where the man who had everything went wrong was in trying to make them do for him what they can never do, seeking in them a kind of fulfilment that they cannot provide. That is the dangerous temptation of affluence and our contempo-rary society has fallen for it in a big way. Because the ordinary pleasures of everyday life are plainly a good thing, the tempta-tion is to think that therefore the accumulation of more and more of them will be even better, that the more one has the more ful-filled one's life will be. The truth is that we only spoil them when we make them the goal of our life's ambition. There is important wisdom in the Teacher's minimalism. It is better to enjoy what we have than to give up that joy in the futile pursuit of more. As the Teacher puts it: 'Better is the sight of the eyes than the wan-dering of desire' (6:9).

But in the end the Teacher leaves us with the negative verdict: it is all meaningless in the end. This is not, of course, the verdict the Bible leaves us with, but it is the role of this one book of the Bible to show us that, viewed from a certain perspective other than that of the gospel, this is what life can look like. It faces us with the question: Have we any real basis for thinking otherwise and living differently? The Teacher's vision of the world is, as we have noticed, astonishingly post-modern. Leave God out, and this is what many people today think. It is the first time in western history that large numbers of people are content to agree with the Teacher that life is ultimately absurd. Moreover, many of them seem content to live accordingly – that is, to live on the surface of life knowing it has no depth, to live in the present knowing there is no future, to divert ourselves by playing life's games knowing there is nothing but the game. It is a fashionable approach, perhaps the dominant trend in our culture, but it trivializes life and spreads a corrosive cynicism through the whole of life.

What would the gospel of Jesus Christ have to say to the Solomon of this book, the man who had everything? This is the man who has tried the pursuit of pleasure and found it to be unfulfilling, who has tried the life of wisdom and found it undermined by death. What was it he was really looking for and could not find? Was he not, in the pursuit of pleasure, seeking something that pursuit could not give him but which really is the fulfilment of human nature? Did he find that there is nothing to be found (the post-modern answer) or only that the pursuit of pleasure is not *where* it is to be found?

What Solomon discovered is that meaning and fulfilment in life are not to be found by getting and having. What the gospel tells us is that they are to be found by receiving and giving. Life and its fullness, meaning and fulfilment in life, are God's gift to us in Christ. They are what we must receive from God and what we must live out in giving of ourselves to God and to others. In a sense we have to fail in order truly to succeed; we have to be losers in order to be winners. We have to fail in the attempt to grasp salvation for ourselves from the things that are within our power – what money can buy, what our intellect can invent. We have to fail in that attempt in order to receive salvation from God and to find the meaning of life in God's giving of himself to us and in our giving of ourselves to God and others. When we find that meaning we find also that it transcends death.

In his letter to the Philippians Paul talks about what he regards as real success in life. If Solomon's story was the story of the man who had everything and found it to be nothing, Paul's story in this passage is the story of the man who gave up everything, knowing it to be nothing:

> Whatever gains I had, these I have come to regard as loss because of Christ. More than that, I regard everything as loss because of the surpassing value of knowing Christ Jesus my Lord. For his sake I have suffered the loss of all things, and I regard them as rubbish, in order that I may gain Christ and be found in him, not having a righteousness of my own that comes from the law, but one that comes through faith in Christ, the righteousness from God based on faith. I want to know Christ and the power of his resurrection and the sharing of his sufferings by becoming like him in his death, if somehow I may attain the resurrection from the dead. Not that I have already obtained this or have already reached the goal; but I press on to make it my own, because Christ Jesus has made me his own (Phil. 3:7-12).

Paul is content to give up the ordinary pursuit of pleasure, power and status for the sake of what really counts, which he calls 'knowing Jesus Christ my Lord'. He is ready to fail, as it were, in order to find the success that God gives – the righteousness that is not his own, not his own achievement, not what he has gained for himself, but the gift of God through faith in Christ. We should notice that this involves a lifelong pursuit, no less than the pursuit of pleasure and material success does. It is a pursuit literally of Christ, following his way of self-giving. It is a pursuit that is not, like Solomon's wisdom, rendered meaningless by death, because it is the pursuit of Christ whom God raised from the dead.

Not the chasing of the wind but the pursuit of Christ. If we ask what is the meaning or fulfilment that the man who had everything was seeking in pleasure and wisdom but could not find, we cannot so much define it as locate it. It is to be found in Jesus

Christ, in knowing God in Christ. We cannot grasp it, for in its fullness it lies ahead of us, but it is to be found in the pursuit of Christ. And just as we can glimpse the emptiness of material success in every achievement that leaves us dissatisfied, so we can glimpse the fullness of life and meaning which is to be had in Christ in every day's experience of living in Christ. Without Christ, all is vanity, meaningless and emptiness. In Christ, everything will find its meaning in the fullness of God.

So the message of our story in the context of the rest of Scripture is: Stop pursuing the wind, pursue Jesus Christ instead.

George Herbert's poem *The Pulley* may help us to know what we should pray for ourselves and for all who are trapped in the disillusioned hedonism of our post-modern culture:

> When God at first made man,
> Having a glass of blessings standing by;
> Let us (said he) pour on him all we can:
> Let the world's riches, which dispersed lie,
> Contract into a span.

> So strength first made a way;
> Then beauty flow'd, then wisdom, honor, pleasure:
> When almost all was out, God made a stay,
> Perceiving that alone of all his treasure
> Rest in the bottom lay.

> For if I should (said he)
> Bestow this jewel also on my creature,
> He would adore my gifts instead of me,
> And rest in Nature, not the God of Nature:
> So both should losers be.

> Yet let him keep the rest,
> But keep them with repining restlessness:
> Let him be rich and weary, that at least,
> If goodness lead him not, yet weariness
> May toss him to my breast.[2]

10

. . . in surprisingly answered prayer

(Isaiah 38)

Sometimes one story provides a helpful avenue to another. So, before we attend to our biblical story, here is a story from modern history. The time is December 1849, the place Semenovsky Square in St Petersburg, Russia. There is deep snow and the air is bitterly cold, but the sun is shining. Among the twenty-eight prisoners who have been brought here is the great Russian writer Fyodor Dostoevsky, who has been tried and held prisoner, along with the others, for his radical political views. The prisoners have only just learned that they have been condemned to die by firing squad. The execution begins at once. Three stakes have been erected in the square, and the first three prisoners are tied to the stakes and their caps are pulled down over their faces. The firing squad is already in line, taking aim and awaiting its officer's command to fire. Dostoevsky is not among the three bound to the stakes, but he will be one of the next three to die. He thinks he has perhaps five minutes left of his life. He begins to make goodbyes to his companions. He focuses on his imminent death, terrified of the unknown prospect it will bring. Perhaps two minutes pass, but two minutes packed with intensified awareness and fear. Then there is a roll of drums, the military signal for retreat. Dostoevsky, himself an ex-army man, realizes at once what this must mean: the sentence is revoked, he will keep his life. The soldiers lower their rifles, the three prisoners are untied, a man arrives riding at a gallop with the Tsar's pardon for the prisoners and the

sentences of exile to Siberia, which replace the death sentence.
It turns out the whole incident has been a deliberate charade.
No execution had been intended, only the Tsar's rather perverse
desire to make the prisoners face the sentence they deserved
before tasting his clemency.

The execution was a mockery, but Dostoevsky's expectation
of imminent death had been agonizingly real, and his reprieve
seemed miraculous, a virtual resurrection, life restored to a
man as good as dead. The experience had a profound and lifelong influence on him. Even though he now faced four years in
the labour camps in Siberia, he found himself ecstatically
happy: 'I cannot recall when I was ever as happy as on that
day,' he said years later. 'I walked up and down my cell . . . and
sang the whole time, sang at the top of my voice, so happy was
I at being given back my life.' It was life as gift he was celebrating, the miracle and blessing of life as sheer gift. It felt like
being born again or rising from the dead, enjoying with new
intensity the life he had previously taken for granted and
squandered. One result of this experience was that he found
himself wanting to love everyone with unconditional love and
forgiveness. It was the root of the special significance he gave in
his novels to the Christian requirement of all-forgiving and all-
embracing love.[1]

Not many people have experienced quite such a confrontation
with death along with so dramatic a reprieve. But one who did
was King Hezekiah of Judah, some two and a half millennia
before Dostoevsky. We shall try to imagine something of
Hezekiah's experience. He was one of the good kings of Judah.
The Old Testament is not complimentary about most of the kings
in Israel's history. Too many of them illustrate the maxim that
power corrupts. Too many of them justified God's warning to his
people, when they insisted on having a king, that they would
live to regret it (1 Sam. 8). But Hezekiah was a good king, his
only apparent fault perhaps that in our story he seems at first a
little too sure of his own goodness. At the time of our story, he
was about forty. He had reigned in Jerusalem for some fifteen
years. Not long before our story takes place, Hezekiah had experienced a stunning intervention of God to rescue his people from
disaster. Jerusalem had been besieged by the army of the

Assyrian king Sennacherib, until one morning 185,000 of Sennacherib's soldiers were found inexplicably dead in their camp outside the city. The only explanation was the word of God that Isaiah had brought to the king, promising that God would defend Jerusalem against the enemy. In this experience Hezekiah had learned both the saving power of God and the trustworthiness of God's prophet Isaiah.

So imagine the effect when Hezekiah falls sick and Isaiah appears at his bedside, with not a word of sympathy or encouragement, but an oracle from the Lord: 'Set your house in order, for you shall die; you shall not recover' (38:1). God had saved Jerusalem from otherwise certain destruction, but Hezekiah he will not save. God himself has sentenced Hezekiah to die. For a man who has learned to trust the word of God on the lips of Isaiah, the prophecy is as convincing and as terrifying as the raised rifles of the firing squad in Dostoevsky's eyes. It is also incomprehensible. What had Hezekiah done to deserve it? So the king's response is to turn on his side on his sickbed, his face to the wall, turning away from the world he must resign himself to leave. Still, accustomed as he is to praying, he cannot but plead with God. The prayer is heartfelt but surely not hopeful. If Hezekiah cannot understand why he must die, nor can he expect God to revoke so definite and unqualified a sentence of death. Hence the title of this chapter: finding God in *unexpectedly answered prayer*. Just as it was for Dostoevsky, so for Hezekiah the shock of totally unexpected reprieve is even greater than the shock of learning he must die.

Isaiah has not even had time to leave the palace before he returns to Hezekiah's sickroom with a new message from God: God has seen Hezekiah's tears. In other words, God has taken notice of Hezekiah's distress and his prayers and has been moved – it seems – to change his mind. He promises to heal Hezekiah. The day after tomorrow the king will be well enough to go to the Temple to give thanks for his recovery. God also repeats his earlier promise to defend Jerusalem, now with Hezekiah himself explicitly included. Hezekiah will live and reign another fifteen years.

Hezekiah cannot believe it. His mind and his emotions cannot cope with this extraordinary reversal of God's judgement. He begins to wonder whether after all he can really trust Isaiah's messages from God. So he asks for a sign that will show this message to be truly from God. This is not too bold a step, because Isaiah was quite well known for the signs from God that sometimes accompanied his prophecies. Clearly Hezekiah is too shattered by his confrontation with imminent death to be able simply to wait two days to see if he really does recover. He wants a sign and he is given one – a sign in its own way just as remarkable as Hezekiah's reprieve from death. God literally puts the clock back. Probably what the story refers to is not a sundial, as some of the translations suggest, but part of the royal palace, a flight of steps known as the steps of king Ahaz, where the sun cast the shadow of a building over the steps. As the sun sank in the sky in the afternoon, the shadow would lengthen, moving down the steps. At the time when Hezekiah and Isaiah are speaking, the shadow has covered ten steps. On this unique day the shadow did not continue to advance down the steps, but turned back the ten steps it had come.

We need not suppose the earth stopped rotating on its axis. An unusual refraction of light in the atmosphere has been suggested. But there is little point in speculating how this sign from God actually occurred. What is important is that this was not just a miracle guaranteeing the truthfulness of Isaiah's prophecy. This was a sign that meant something. Like the signs Jesus performs in John's Gospel (which calls Jesus' miracles 'signs'), this sign signifies something greater than itself. As the shadow moves back ten steps, so God is giving Hezekiah fifteen years of life that he could never have counted on, fifteen years gratuitously added into the calendar, fifteen years of God's sheer gift of life to a man who was as good as dead. Hezekiah has what people usually only wish for as a counterfactual supposition: 'if I had my time over again.' Hezekiah actually has his time over again, his fifteen-year reign all over again, to be lived now with just that heightened sense of the miracle of life that Dostoevsky had even in Siberia.

Dostoevsky, we remember, was so ecstatic with joy he sang – and could not stop singing. Similarly Hezekiah sang. He even composed a song to sing in the Temple. It is a song about coming back from the dead. He recalls what it felt like to suffer God's sentence of death, finding himself at the very gates of Sheol, the place of the dead, taking leave of the world of the living, reaching nightfall already in the noontide of his life. His instinct is to plead for his life to God, 'but,' he says, 'what can I say? For he has spoken to me, and he himself has done it' (38:15). Surely the sentence is irrevocable, and yet he prays: 'Oh, restore me to health and make me live!' (38:16). We need to recall that Hezekiah will have had no belief in life with God after death. The hope of resurrection after death began to dawn only later in the Old Testament period. So he can say:

> For Sheol cannot thank you,
> death cannot praise you;
> those who go down to the Pit cannot hope for your
> faithfulness.
> The living, the living, they thank you, as I do this day;
> fathers make known to children your faithfulness. (38:18-19)

For Hezekiah life is about thanking and praising God. The fact that life itself, as Dostoevsky also discovered, is sheer gift of God, a daily miracle, something to be ecstatic about, means that the praise of God is the fullest expression of being truly alive. The dead cannot praise God, but 'the living, the living' (Hezekiah repeats the word with the amazement of someone who had not expected still to be one of them) . . . 'the living, the living, they give thanks to you, as I do this day' (with the astonishment still in his voice). What then will it be like to have his time all over again: 'we will sing to stringed instruments all the days of our lives at the house of the LORD' (38:20). In this jubilant conclusion to his song, Hezekiah is not thinking he *ought* to be thankful. What he expresses is spontaneous joy in life experienced as given back, as life received from God, life experienced as doubly good when it is experienced as God's gift, life truly lived because no longer taken for granted, life as what we hardly dare pray for and can never presume on, life as praise.

We find a remarkable contemporary expression of this experience in the poem, *Twofold*, by the Irish Christian poet Micheal O'Siadhail:

Fit. Summered. Thoughtful. Balanced. Urbane.
Broken as a reed in bending humiliations of pain.
Has a world ever been so carefree, so debonair,
That morning you fetched me from Intensive Care?
Trees, touch of your hand, colour of your blouse,
Snatches of street-talk, hues of a pink-bricked house.

A first walk in the garden linking you my Eve;
Your body as it curved to pick up a fallen leaf.

Richer and richer and richer. My endless paradise.
But more than to seize the day, to hold it twice!

A moment doubly relishing its tang and flavour.
Once just to taste and once more to savour.

Folding intensity of living in the light of mortality.
And yes! half of what we love is love's fragility.

Will this morning be that morning all over again?
Coward that I am, I still praise. Amen. Amen.

Looped awareness vibrates like a twofold rhyme.
Sweet density. And I want to live in double time.[2]

O'Siadhail's notion of living in double time is a kind of image of life not taken for granted, like Dostoevsky's ecstatic joy in knowing life to be gift, like Hezekiah's sense of life lived over again in praise of the God who gives it. For O'Siadhail it is the 'folded intensity of living in the light of mortality', and it is also 'my endless Paradise', a kind of Eden to which he wants again and again to return.

Since telling Dostoevsky's story, we have been using terms like resurrection, new birth, life given back to the virtually dead, return to Eden. These are terms that come readily to those who have such experiences and find God in them. The better we know life to be sheer gift of God, the more sense it will make to us to believe God's promise of resurrection for not just the virtually dead but even the actually dead. Or, conversely, the more we live in the light of God's promise of resurrection, given to us in the resurrection of Jesus, the more we shall experience daily life as God's gift, not to be taken *for* granted but taken *as* granted by God, received again and again from the generous giver of all good. We shall find this God of life and resurrection in many a reminder of loss and mortality out of which God renews life.

Hezekiah's story is just one of a series of Old Testament stories of life given back out of virtual death: Abraham in agonizing obedience to God gives up his son for dead and beyond expectation receives him back; Joseph is given up for dead by his family and given back to them with blessings they could never have expected; Shadrach, Meshach and Abednego experience God's deliverance only when they are prepared, if he lets them, to die for him; Jonah famously accomplishes his mission as God's prophet only when he sinks to a watery grave and the sea monster vomits him back onto the shore; and many a psalmist tells of being delivered by God from the very jaws of death in one form or another. (Hezekiah's own psalm is in fact one of many rather similar ones in the book of Psalms.) Each of these stories is very different; they are not at all repetitive; and we maybe would not even see a connection between them if we did not see them with the hindsight given to readers of the New Testament. But once we see the connection, we can recognize the recurrent theme reappearing through all the differences. And we may only grasp the full significance of Hezekiah's story only when we see that it is one of this series of these coming-back-from-the-virtually-dead stories.

The significance of these stories is not just that as Christian believers in the resurrection of Jesus we can see it prefigured already in the Old Testament. It is also that they encourage us to recognize the God of the resurrection in God's ways with us in our lives this side of death. In loss and renewal, in giving up and receiving back we find the God who raised Jesus from the dead. We may not experience dramatic instances of this, like the biblical ones or like Dostoevsky's experience, but in many smaller ways we can find the same pattern in our own lives. God brings us to points where we give up, cannot see how we can go on, lose what seems irreplaceably precious, or just find life joyless and hopeless. From time to time all of us turn our faces to the wall or are tempted to. Then we pray not expecting answers. In such cases God's answers are rarely what we expect. In surprisingly answered prayers we find the God who exceeds our expectations. The God who surprised the disciples on Easter morning can certainly surprise us in many less miraculous ways. In such surprises we find the joy of life itself as God's gift, as living in double time, as praise of God.

But of Hezekiah's story there is a further aspect to be observed: the way it points beyond itself to something greater. Among all the Old Testament's coming-back-from-the-virtually-dead stories, this one is unique in the startling sign given to the king: the shadow cast by the sun turns back. This is a sign that seems to overleap its immediate meaning as a sign for Hezekiah about his own fifteen-year reprieve, remarkable enough though that was. Surely it has a surplus of significance that points to something even greater? God puts the clock back. The irreversibility of time is more or less the only thing we really know about that mysterious medium in which we all live our whole lives. 'You can't turn the clock back' is a popular formulation of this basic truth of our world. In time all things pass away, our lives slip into the past, even memories fade, our loved ones die, every joy passes, and we ourselves will come to the end of our lives. Time is relentlessly one-directional. We cannot have the past back. We cannot have the dead back. We cannot have our own lives back; we cannot come back from the dead.

But Hezekiah's sign hints – and this is surely why we find it so strange and hard to believe, even by comparison with many another biblical miracle – that time is not irreversible for God. The hint is surely of resurrection and new creation, the hope, given us when God raised Jesus from death, that God will in the end not let the creation he loves be lost forever, but will indeed turn the cosmic clock back. Then God will reverse the sentence of death he has passed on us all, the fate of mortality that comes to all things in time. Then God will give us back our lives to live quite newly and differently in the ecstasy of eternal joy. Then we shall return to the endless Eden and live in the double time of resurrection life. Then we shall live in uninterrupted praise of God. Meantime, knowing that with God that is possible and shall be, we find even in our temporal and mortal lives now the life that will not be lost because it is God's gift.

Lord, when our lives seem predictable
you are the unpredictable one.
When we take life for granted
you are the shock or the surprise –
or, best of all, both –
that gives us back life's giftedness.
You are the moment-by-moment giver
of the lives we imagine our own
and yours it is to give excessively
beyond what we imagine.
God of life, living God,
truly to live is to praise you!
God of life, ever-living God,
truly to live will be to praise you forever!

11

... in resisting idolatry

(Daniel 3)

Nebuchadnezzar's great golden statue was no less than ninety feet high. People in Nebuchadnezzar's empire were used to huge images of their gods, but we can be sure no one would have seen an image that tall before. It was even bigger than the famous Colossus of Rhodes, one of the wonders of the ancient world. Nebuchadnezzar's golden statue was meant to outdo all others. It was meant to impress. The book of Daniel does not tell us which god it was meant to represent. Most likely it was Bel the patron deity of Babylon, but perhaps it was some newly invented deity whose cult Nebuchadnezzar had decided to initiate. It may be that the author very deliberately has not told us, because more important than the particular god it might be supposed to be is the fact that really the statue personified Nebuchadnezzar's power, the spirit of Babylon, the greatness of Nebuchadnezzar's empire. Nebuchadnezzar, who – with some degree of exaggeration – boasted that he ruled the whole world (see Dan. 4:1), wanted to impress his subjects with this image of his power and glory. Its purpose was just as much political as it was religious. It represented Nebuchadnezzar's power as godlike, absolute, reaching like the tower of Babel up to the very heavens.

Nebuchadnezzar knew something every astute politician knows. He knew that if his vast, disparate empire was to hold together, if it was to form a cohesive political unity, it was not sufficient to have efficient administrative structures for governing the empire and armies ready to put down rebellions. The empire needed an inspirational focus of loyalty and common purpose. It needed a common commitment to some kind of ideal. It needed – at least in the ancient world this was the obvious form for such a thing to take – a religious focus. People's religious instincts to admire and to serve something greater than themselves needed focusing on the empire. And so the dedication of the statue was a great festival of political religion.

Anyone who can remember the days of the Soviet Union will remember the annual May Day parade in Red Square in Moscow, a great celebration of the power of the Soviet Union, designed to impress. Much the same kind of pomp and circumstance attends Nebuchadnezzar's great dedication festival. All the dignitaries, officials and civil servants from the whole empire are summoned to attend. Rank and protocol are scrupulously observed, as the writer laboriously tells us: 'the satraps, the prefects, and the governors, the counsellors, the treasurers, the justices, the magistrates, and all the officials of the provinces' (3:2). No doubt they are all attired in their robes of office. Here is the state at all its levels assembled in magnificent array. The orchestra too is impressive. After the preliminaries of the ceremony, the herald mounts the stage and with a voice trained to carry even across a vast assembly of people like this, he proclaims: 'You are commanded, O peoples, nations, and languages, that when you hear the sound of the horn, pipe, lyre, trigon, harp, drum, and entire musical ensemble, you are to fall down and worship the golden statue that king Nebuchadnezzar has set up' (3:4-5).

You will have noticed that the writer of Daniel 3 is rather fond of such lists. He makes them sound like incantations with some kind of power in the mere enunciation of the words. The elaborate list of dignitaries he gives twice (3:2, 3). The list of the musical instruments he repeats no less than four times in the chapter (3:5, 7, 10, 15). On the first occasion he is no doubt giving his readers a sense of the dazzling magnificence of the occasion. Who could fail to be impressed, cowed even, overpowered by it all, even if they were otherwise inclined to be less than enthusiastic about the festival? Who could fail to be caught up by the music into the spirit of awed reverence it was meant to induce? But when the writer repeats the lists, we get a rather different impression. It begins to sound as though all this huffing and puffing is being mocked. There is evidently a perspective from which it all looks like a rather silly charade. It is all pretension without real substance. But if the writer is in fact subtly inviting us to deride Nebuchadnezzar and to deconstruct all this pomp and circumstance, how is such a perspective available? Surely anyone in that crowd would have thought Nebuchadnezzar's power real enough. When the herald ends his proclamation with a warning – that if anyone refuses to worship, he 'shall immediately be thrown into a furnace of blazing fire' (3:6) – everyone knows that is no empty threat. Nebuchadnezzar has the power to do just that. So if the great show of power fails to impress, should one not nevertheless be obliged to concede that there is no alternative but to go along with it? In due course the chapter will open up for us the perspective from which it is possible to refuse to take seriously Nebuchadnezzar's inflated ceremonial. For the moment, we might remember a striking passage in the second psalm, one of the few passages in Scripture where God is said to laugh. The psalm depicts a great conspiracy of the rulers of the world, gathered together in all their might to challenge God's power over them. But (says the psalmist) the one 'who sits in the heavens laughs them to scorn; the LORD has them in derision' (Ps. 2:4).

However, this divine mockery is not shared by those involved in Nebuchadnezzar's dedication festival. For them it fulfils its function as one of those great symbolic occasions that binds a society together in commitment to a common ideal. Societies always seek some common focus of values, and very often in the past that has taken religious form: a state religion that focuses people's loyalty to the state. The strength of such commitment to a common ideal can show itself in the fact that nonconformists – the people who refuse to join in – cannot be tolerated. This is the main reason religious minorities often get persecuted. It is the reason even societies that called themselves Christian persecuted groups like the Jews. The history of such Christian intolerance and cruelty is so shocking that we prefer not to remember it, but it was possible because people thought of Christianity as the cement that bound society together, the focus of common values. Anyone who did not join in the state religion was a threat. It was for the same reason that Christians were persecuted in the Roman Empire and very often down to the present time. Christians, with an ultimate loyalty to God and God's values, are often and ought often to be nonconformists. They are people who cannot give unquestioning loyalty to what their society holds dear.

This does not normally mean opting out and taking no part in society. In extreme cases it means that, but not usually. The story in Daniel 3 is not about people who opted out but about people who are involved in society at the highest political level. They are called Shadrach, Meshach and Abednego, which were not their original, Jewish names, but their new Babylonian names, given them when Nebuchadnezzar took them into his service and gave them high-ranking posts in the government of the empire (Dan. 1:6-7). Here are people trying to be faithful to God at the heart of the government of a pagan empire. If they had not held prominent government positions, their absence from the great dedication ceremony would not have been noticed. They were important people. But they had to draw the line, at whatever cost, because, although they served Nebuchadnezzar as their king, they did not serve him as their god.

Perhaps Nebuchadnezzar himself, with plenty else on his mind, would not have noticed their absence, had it not been drawn to his attention by other members of his court who were no doubt envious of the three Jews and seized with relish the opportunity to denounce them. They were easy targets: outsiders, members of a conquered nation, with no access to power and influence other than the king's own favour. Powerful they might be as servants of Nebuchadnezzar the king, but once denounced as disloyal, once deprived of Nebuchadnezzar's favour, they are completely powerless and vulnerable. But they have no choice – or they have only the choice which idolatry always presents to God's people, the choice between the true god and the false. Nebuchadnezzar himself confronts them with the choice as a choice of gods. Pompously repeating the herald's message in case they have failed to take it in, he repeats the threat and adds a gloss of his own: 'But if you do not worship, you will immediately be thrown into a furnace of blazing fire, and who is the god that will deliver you out of my hands?' (3:15) It is clear now that Nebuchadnezzar's great golden statue is no more nor less than the deification of his own power. It stands as an unmistakable challenge to any other god that might claim to rival his power. For Nebuchadnezzar gods are like kings, contending for supremacy. Having seen off all his rivals on earth, Nebuchadnezzar, with his heaven-high idol, is now engaged in challenging any other gods there might be in heaven. Is there any who can deliver from his hand those he chooses to put to excruciating death?

In Israel's traditions the one who claimed that 'no one can deliver from my hand' was the God of Israel, the Most High God. It was this God who, in Deuteronomy 32:39, proclaimed his absolute uniqueness in such terms:

> See now, that I, even I, am he;
> there is no god besides me.
> I kill and I make alive;
> I wound and I heal;
> and no one can deliver from my hand.

Who then truly has the power over life and death: Nebuchadnezzar or the Most High, the God of Israel? Faced with that challenge, what can Shadrach, Meshach and Abednego do but what they actually do? Yet what courage it demands of them. They have nothing to say except to leave the matter in the hands of their God. 'Whatever happens,' they say, 'whether our God delivers us from the furnace or not, we want you to know, O king, that we will not serve your gods and we will not worship the image of gold that you have set up' (cf. 3:17-19). This is extraordinary faith.

We might have thought that men of such faith would count on God's deliverance. What sort of God is this who commands the loyalty of his people even if he fails to prove himself God in the face of Nebuchadnezzar's challenge? Even if to all appearances Nebuchadnezzar proves to be supreme, even if they perish in the furnace, Shadrach, Meshach and Abednego cannot but acknowledge this God to be the true God. At this moment their God looks as weak and vulnerable as they. But nevertheless in the loyalty of his people to him it becomes clear that this God is a God to be taken far more seriously than Nebuchadnezzar's ridiculously glittering colossus, whose worship has to be enforced by threats. Worshipping Nebuchadnezzar's god is obvious self-interest.

Genuinely impressed or not, everyone bows down to save their skin or to advance their prospects in Nebuchadnezzar's service. Nebuchadnezzar's cult is the way to get on, while staying loyal to the God of Israel obviously is not. Yet it is from this perspective of loyalty to the true God, even without knowing whether he will rescue his people or not, that all the impressive paraphernalia of Nebuchadnezzar's cult appear absurdly implausible. The idol towers above its worshippers, but even the birds fly higher. What kind of a threat can it appear from heaven?

Was it only ancient societies or only societies subject to tyranny that have fallen for this kind of ludicrous idolatry? Far from it. All societies need common values and ideals, and probably more often than not (even if explicitly religious terms are not used) that focus of common commitment becomes an idol. It is idolatry when it is treated as something that may not be questioned, something that takes precedence over everything else, an object of ultimate trust and obedience, something for which anything else may be sacrificed and to dissent from which is not tolerated. For example, there are idols of militarism, nationalism and power. It is not difficult to identify these idols, with their insatiable bloodlust for sacrifice, captivating many in the world today. These are ancient and modern idols from which we are never safe.

There is also a more seductive idol abroad in the world and dominant in Western society. We have little enough in the way of common values left in most Western societies. But if there is one overriding common commitment that dominates political life and economic life, family and individual life, it is surely the commitment to ever-increasing affluence and material prosperity. This is an idol that shows itself to be an idol especially in being unquestionable: unquestionable in politics, unquestionable in the media. The liturgies and ceremonies of its cult are all around us daily. The axiom of constantly increasing material consumption is an idol not only because it is unquestionable and not only because it is so dominant in all areas of life, but also because it seduces people in a way that blinds us to its obvious destructiveness and futility. Idols always seem both impressive and attractive. Because of their attraction we do not really want to know the damage they do. We can say that economic growth is the only way to better education, better health care and other clearly desirable goals, but we forget that it is also – and mostly – about rampant consumerism: persuading people they cannot do without things they never dreamed of wanting until someone decided to market them. We forget that it is about the commercialization of much that used to be free, and we forget that it threatens the planet and the lives of people who will never share the prosperity we enjoy at their expense. The straightforward fact that the planet cannot support a whole world of people consuming resources at the rate we in the affluent West do seems powerless against the idol of consumerism. Perhaps it is time that we in the Christian churches confronted the choice that idolatry always forces. In one sense it is harder for us than for Shadrach, Meshach and Abednego. They confronted a single make-or-break choice. For us there are a myriad daily choices in which a decision for God rather than the idol of consumerism has to be taken. On the other hand, most of these choices – at least the ones with which we need to begin if we are to take the issue seriously at all – are far less demanding of courage than theirs.

Jesus said: 'No one can serve two masters; for a slave will either hate the one and love the other, or be devoted to the one and despise the other. You cannot serve God and Mammon' (Matt. 6:24). The word 'mammon' means money or material possessions, but Jesus uses it as though it were the name for a god. As a rival for the loyalty we owe to the one true God it is indeed an idol. So for ourselves, perhaps, we could usefully give the name Mammon to Nebuchadnezzar's nameless golden image. Let's begin to see the cult of affluence for the deceptive charade it is, never delivering what it promises. Let's start mocking it. Let's attune our ears to the derisive laughter from heaven that cuts every idol down to size. Sharing God's ridicule of the pretensions of idols is a not a bad way to start resisting them.

For *resistance* is precisely what is needed – with all the overtones of bravery and intelligence that the idea of wartime resistance gives to that word. In a society dominated by idols, God's people are in territory under enemy occupation. Resistance requires daily vigilance, tactical ingenuity and long-term strategic thinking. But the promise of Daniel 3, in the end of the story that we have still to mention, is that it is in such resistance that we shall find God with us. There is a passage in Isaiah which could very appropriately have been in the minds of Shadrach, Meshach and Abednego, had they remembered it as they faced the fiery furnace. God addresses Israel:

> Do not fear, for I have redeemed you;
> I have called you by name, you are mine.
> When you pass through the waters, I will be with you;
> and through the rivers, they shall not overwhelm you;
> when you walk through fire you shall not be burned,
> and the flame will not consume you (Isa. 43:1-2).

What happened to Shadrach, Meshach and Abednego was a kind of dramatic illustration of that promise. Of course, God does not always keep his people physically safe, and Shadrach, Meshach and Abednego did not, as we have seen, require him to. They were loyal to God – full stop. They set no conditions of being rescued. But God does promise that, whenever his people suffer in their resistance to idolatry, he is in it with them. The most important thing God did for Shadrach, Meshach and Abednego was not to deliver them from death, but to enable them not to succumb to Nebuchadnezzar's gods. As a result Nebuchadnezzar himself was impressed, far more impressed than anyone was by his golden image. He was impressed not just by the miraculous fact that the three were unharmed by the fire, but by the fact that he saw four men, not three, walking in the fire, and recognized the fourth as the God of Israel, the Most High God, walking with his people. When God's people resist the idols of society, refusing, whatever the cost, to serve the golden image, and when people see the true God with them in that resistance, that is when God's people make an impact in God's world.

> God Most High,
> there are idols that seem to rule in our world
> and daily demand our obeisance.
> They seduce us with their glittering lure
> and we fail to notice the destruction they deal to others
> or the trap they set for ourselves.
> They impress us with pomp and power
> and all too easily we agree
> that there is no alternative.

But you alone are the Most High God.
Supreme above their empty posturing
you have them in derision.
Give us the courage to defy them
and the wit to outwit them.
We do not expect it to be easy.
We may even find ourselves in the furnace,
but we know that, there above all, you will be with us,
and that even when it hurts like hell
the flame shall not harm us,
because you walk with us in the furnace.

Notes

Foreword
[1] C. S. Lewis, *An Experiment in Criticism* (Cambridge: Cambridge University Press, 1961), pp. 139-41.

2 . . . in the loneliness of life's journey
[1] Francis Thomson, *Selected Poems* (London: Methuen/Burns & Oates, 1910), pp. 130-1.

4 . . . in the stupidity born of anger
[1] See E. M. Forster, *Aspects of the Novel* (London: Pelican, 1962), pp. 75ff.
[2] Eugene Peterson, *The Message of David* (London: Marshall Pickering, 1997), p. 81f.
[3] Modern translations amend the reference here to David's enemies as being in fact to David himself, which strengthens rather than weakens the rhetorical point of the oath.

5 . . . in the clutches of sin
[1] 'Out of my Soul's Depth' by Thomas Campion (1567–1620) from Lord David Cecil (ed.), *The Oxford Book of Christian Verse* (Oxford: Clarendon Press, 1940), pp. 74-5.

6 . . . in the pride born of influence
[1] Extract from 'Lord, it belongs not to my Care' by Richard Baxter (1615–91), in Lord David Cecil (ed.), *The Oxford Book of Christian Verse* (Oxford: Clarendon Press, 1940), p. 217.

9 . . . in the futility of success

[1] W. B. Yeats, *Selected Poetry*, ed. A. N. Jeffares (London: Pan, 1974), p. 184.

[2] George Herbert, *The Country Parson, The Temple*, ed. J. N. Wall (Classics of Western Spirituality; New York: Paulist, 1981) pp. 284-5.

10 . . . in surprisingly answered prayer

[1] This account is based on Joseph Frank, *Dostoevsky: The Years of Ordeal 1850–1859* (Princeton: Princeton University Press, 1983), chapter 5.

[2] Micheal O'Siadhail, *Our Double Time* (Newcastle upon Tyne: Bloodaxe Books, 1998), p. 24.